STUDIES IN ENGLISH LITERATURE

Volume LIV

CONRAD'S COLONIALISM

by

ROBERT F. LEE
The College of Steubenville

1969

MOUTON

THE HAGUE · PARIS

LIBRARY OF CONGRESS CATALOG CARD NUMBER: 68-30868

Printed in The Netherlands by Mouton & Co., Printers, The Hague.

For three young people who have greatly delighted and enriched my life:

> *Rashid Soufi,*
> *James G. Crowley,*
> *and*
> *Nancy Lee Hutchin*

TABLE OF CONTENTS

INTRODUCTION

The purpose of this critical study is to examine Joseph Conrad's colonial *milieu* by close and specific reference to his following works: *Almayer's Folly; An Outcast of the Islands; Heart of Darkness; Lord Jim; The Nigger of the Narcissus; Nostromo: A Tale of the Seaboard; The Rescue; Typhoon; Victory;* "An Outpost of Progress"; "Because of the Dollars"; "Karain: A Memory"; "The Lagoon"; and "The Planter of Malata".

Correlative material from some of his other works is utilized to support the interpretation of the preceding fiction which is to have the major consideration.[1]

The examination of the above fiction is offered under the general considerations set forth in the Table of Contents. Certainly the narrow concern of the following evaluations does not completely explain Conrad's greatness as an artist, which lies quite rightly in the universality of his view of life and his ability to express that view. However, there are themes in his works which, by a fuller knowledge and understanding of his attitudes toward colonialism as he thought of it, are made sharper, brighter, and clearer. A fuller knowledge and understanding also allow a razor-

---

[1] All quotations, unless otherwise noted, will be made from the Doubleday, Page and Company 1924 edition of Joseph Conrad's *Complete Works*. Acknowledgments are made with thanks to the Trustees of the Joseph Conrad Estate, Doubleday and Company as publishers of Conrad's work in the U.S.A., and J. M. Dent and Sons Ltd. as publishers of the volumes in England and agents for the Trustees of the Joseph Conrad Estate.

edge interpretation for an audience of today, who even though removed by only a few years in time, are removed vastly from the climate of opinion and the factual information of another part of the world existing in Conrad's era. Conrad's terms and attitudes may not be those of our own time; and this study will make no attempt to contrast or compare ethically his terms and attitudes to the general values held today concerning race, nationalism, and sovereignty of one group over another, or of one individual over others, but will attempt only to make them available.

It would be difficult to deny that since World War II some of the greatest social changes, both in philosophy and in practice, have occurred in the Orient. It may also be difficult to realize unconsciously that very little change had occurred in the Orient for some sixty years prior to World War II, in comparison to the rest of the highly civilized world; for we certainly may recognize the Orient, though different from the West, as one of the most highly civilized areas for many past hundreds, even thousands of years. Therefore, even though this work will not deal expansively with the qualities of universal greatness in Conrad's works *per se,* those qualities will naturally come under consideration when their embellishments are looked at. To reiterate, it is expected that the reader realize the subject of this investigation does not presume to stand as the central worth of Conrad, but will, it is hoped, throw extra light on and make more available for appreciation, the greatness of Conrad's theme of man's identity.

One of the major directions of Conrad's colonial fiction is a recognition of and an accord with the conception of Anglo-Saxon superiority in administering lives of Oriental and other dependent peoples. But Conrad keeps his main artistic concerns on the individual man, no matter what general racial or national qualities he may believe in. By displaying this innate superior administrative ability in the actions and thoughts of merchant adventurers, rather than in the conventional characterization of official personages, whom his works indicate he disapproves of, Conrad is able to show the virtues of courage, objective justice, assumption of responsibilities, and trustworthiness operating not under the controlling shadow of a puissant State Government, but effecting control independently over the people of a philosophy alien to that of his heroes.

Though neither group fully – nor often even nearly – understands the other, the dependent peoples continually and voluntarily turn with complex and torturing confidence to the British – Conrad's representation of the highest achievement of administrative ability among white men – for the solution to problems which arise from the intricacies of their own *milieu*. Forced by the drive of his own instincts, the white man, even when not asked, must accept the responsibility of aiding and guiding the dependent peoples even though he knows there will never be any genuine reward other than his own realization of carrying out the dictates of his destiny.

The subtle oppressions, the subtle and not so subtle failures and betrayals of such a destiny, as developed by Conrad, add the tragic stature to his work and view of life and keep the stories from the crassness of mere romantic tales of a far-flung Empire. In addition to the oppressions and betrayals, the lack of gratitude and appreciation by the East for the genuine benefits derived from the white man is another of the negative aspects of Conrad's treatment of the white man's burden. However, Conrad's concern with the depressing and vigorous pessimism of his subject, powerful as it is, never overwhelms his conviction that the "burden", like life, must be assumed if the white man is to remain true to others, true to his own, and true to himself.

* * *

To make the all-inclusive generalization that one race or one people is better than others is unwise; but, even in the face of the omnipresent danger of any generality, it is also unwise to reject the concept that a race or a people possesses or demonstrates superiority over others in one or more phases or aspects of life. To compare the Gentoo Law Code of the Hindu culture to the body of law of the American Indian would be poor judgment. To compare the architectural attainments of the South African Negro to that of the Aztec would be unreasonable. To compare the sense of civic organization of the pre-communist state of the Chinese to that of the Japanese would be as unjustified as comparing the sense of humor of the inhabitants of Japan to that sublime trait in the people of China. It can be concluded from his works that Conrad believes a panoramic examination of history shows that in judicial and administrative control of other peoples, the superiority of the Anglo-Saxon – even though he himself was not one – has never been excelled. Being as perceptive an artist as he is, he does not claim their control has been perfect or they could have done no better. He does foster the opinion that in a wide scope examination up to his time, no other people have indicated an ability equal to the British in matters of judicial administration on a basis considered ethical by Western standards.

Conrad himself realized that he was dealing in themes which might well escape the reader; for, as Guerard points out, "Conrad never ceased to complain of the average reader: of his obtuse failure to see, beneath adventure and sentiment, behind explicit statement, a region of complex intention." [2] In Conrad's own words, he was opposed to "that obsession of my sea-life, which has about as much bearing on my literary existence, on my quality as a writer, as the enumeration of drawing rooms which Thackeray frequented could have had on his gift as a great novelist".[3] But such complaining may not be entirely justified when the vehicles for the "region of complex intention" utilize an exotic, romantic, and strange *milieu* dependent for full appreciation upon understanding of climates of opinion, times, and situations neither universal, nor readily available to the general reader. Conrad as a creative artist certainly does not need defense for using comparatively unavailable settings for his themes, for his works are not intended as source material for "social studies" in the academic sense, anymore than they are intended as pure adventure stories. Of course so much of his Oriental background is a part of him that he unconsciously involves his reader in material quite foreign to the Western man. In the same foreign atmosphere, the Western reader can be brought up short by reading, through the inter-

[2]   Albert Guerard, Jr., "Joseph Conrad", *Directions*, Number 1 (New York, New Directions, 1947), p. 10.
[3]   *Ibid.*, p. 12.

pretation of an Eastern or Oriental character, concrete statements of Western beliefs and practices which the reader has known only in a vague or semiconscious way because they make up an imbued part of his own Western culture.

Since the white man's burden does not now exist as a popular philosophy or a general practice in all those areas of the world brought under Anglo-Saxon control in the past three hundred years, it will be difficult – very likely impossible – within a short time, to obtain first-hand and true information concerning the operation of the "burden" in the East. The Orient has already refuted its relations with Great Britain in many ways indicative of mental operations somewhat beyond Western rational understanding. In 1951, the Indian government in Calcutta (through no sense of guilt) removed the monument to the dead from the site of the "Black Hole of Calcutta", thereby enabling some well-educated and truly sophisticated Indians to claim sincerely that the incident never occurred. They insisted that the monument was no more than a fabricated British indignity.[4]

There is evident in some of the recent critical publications on Conrad a lack of knowledge of the East which results in appraisal and appreciation either not complete or not quite true. It is understandable that the same authors of those critical works would find unsettling, if not somewhat incomprehensible, the case of the leader of an Eastern nation who appeared in this

---

[4] The situation took place during my residence in India. I have taken the liberty to draw on personal experiences in a few places in this study as they sometimes allow a comparatively closer and more revealing examination of ethnocentric attitudes than do experiences taken out of books. Because of my interest in the East, I was well aware during my nine and one-half years' background in the Philippine Islands, China, Japan, Hawaii, Okinawa, Ceylon, India, Pakistan, Egypt, and Burma, that I had an unusual opportunity to observe artistic, economic, political, and social phases of that part of the world. Persons have been deliberately left unidentified by name, as many are still in prominent national positions. The long and unusual conversation concerning the removal of the monument for the "Black Hole of Calcutta" took place at tea with Shewbux Satyanarain Bajoria, Esq., a remarkable Mawari business potentate, who was held in high esteem by his Bengali guests because of his mastery of their language and knowledge of their literature. I was the only European present. (Any white man is classified as a European, no matter what continent he may come from.)

country in 1951. His appearance in complete European dress (a matter of constant and pointed attack by him in his homeland) was before an international diplomatic audience to talk on the mutual benefits of East-West cooperation. He had previously addressed – in English, since he is not as proficient in his mother tongue – his own Parliament to explain his national budget for the coming year in terms of import duties being not only a source of income, but also "a means of punishing foreigners"! His speeches outside of his homeland were so different as to gain for himself the acclaim by the innocent weekly magazines in the United States that he was one of the most competent diplomats at the conference. They paid him more due than they knew. In his country, among embassy and government groups, he was known as "The Snake".

A certain amount of confusion would exist in attempting to evaluate the supreme leader of another, and great, Oriental nation, who, addressing thousands of his countrymen on peace, in English (which only a negligible percentage of the group understood), stepped off the speaker's platform to strike a member of the audience in the face for talking with his neighbor during the speech. In still another Eastern country a great businessman – knighted by the British Crown in recognition of his prominence – insisted that a contract for an important matter be signed at an exact moment after 4:00 o'clock on a Sunday morning by his legal agents, a well-known British firm, since the stars showed that particular time to be the most auspicious hour for concluding the transaction. Those same stars indicated as late as 1948 to the court astrologers of Burma that the signing of the constitution would have to be delayed, since the heavens were then not completely propitious.

Under no circumstances are these examples being offered disparagingly; such a presentation would be a blatant failure. They do enhance the insistence that the atmosphere surrounding Eastern life must be taken into full consideration before a somewhat complete appreciation of Conrad can be experienced.

The above incidents took place within a few recent years, 1947-1951. They have been deliberately drawn from the highest social and governmental elements in those lands in order that the reader can consider what even stranger attitudes existed about eighty years ago – and how much more intensified those attitudes were, and are, in levels of Eastern society less cosmopolitan and more ethnocentric.

It may be difficult for Mr. Albert Guerard, Jr. to assimilate the fabulousness of Conrad's *milieu*, in which the white man's burden and its effects on the men involved constitute a major avenue of understanding. In any case he is unable to accept as life-like the fact that Heemskirk, in "Freya of the Seven Isles", becomes so angry that he momentarily is blind with rage, or that Almayer,[5] Williams,[6] and Linguard [7] are all subject to fits of temper.[8]

An Irish executive of a British firm, a friend of the writer of this study, upon ordering food to be prepared late one evening, received an impertinent reply from his cook. He proceeded with a butcher knife to chase that cook for many blocks through the capital of Ceylon. It may be admitted that there was loss of dignity on both sides (cooks being a high rank of servant); it must be admitted that there was anger – anger which resulted in action possibly quite foreign in New England but which nevertheless was very life-like and lively!

To turn to a more revealing and more serious example of a domestic atmosphere foreign to our area but not our time, we may consider the incident which started with Mr. A's returning home and being informed that one of the young male house servants had interfered with an *ayah*, a female servant. The fact that the house boy was taken to the back compound, tied to a tree, and whipped in disgrace did not surprise any of us. Physical punishment of servants by native residents is common, whereas it is not among Europeans in the East. What did come as a shock was the knowledge that Mr. A had engineered the whole execution by himself; for we had always known him as a small, gentle, refined, retiring although very capable lawyer. In fact, he was extremely

---

[5]   *Almayer's Folly, An Outcast of the Islands.*
[6]   *An Outcast of the Islands.*
[7]   *The Rescue, An Outcast of the Islands, Almayer's Folly.*
[8]   Guerard, p. 26.

well liked by all because of what is seldomly found anywhere, a
sweet nature. But anger at having the rules of his renownedly
well-ordered household broken was so extreme that it not only
changed his whole personality momentarily, but obviously gave
him an unusual physical advantage over a larger and younger
man. The other fascination of the occurrence was this question:
What was the important point of the whole matter? It was not the
beating, as we Occidentals might imagine, but the banishing of
the servant from Colombo to his village in the hills, where he
would live with the ever-present stigma that he had been ejected
for gross misconduct from a household well known for its decorum. It is in such an atmosphere of strong beliefs, from domestic
to government levels, that we find ourselves when involved in
Conrad's works.

Guerard falls into what may be a legitimate error in his elabo-
ration on Gustav Morf's argument that Conrad's attractive portrait of Lord Jim was unconscious compensation for his own slight
physique.[9] However, in *The Seas Were Mine*,[10] the author, a
sea-captain who knew Conrad, describes an actual Lord Jim. He
appears about the same as Conrad presents him as far as physical
aspect is concerned. In Captain Hartman's account, Jim, though
handsome, was something of a fop and sported a monocle! He
at one time stole a native girl from his uncle and ran away with
her. To keep his uncle from giving chase, he also stole his ship. He
had not, therefore, the personality of Jim of the novel, even though
he may have had the same outward form.

Guerard gives the impression in many of his comments that he
has forgotten Conrad had seen a great deal of the world and life,
and had seen it in the responsible position of a ship's officer of
eighty years ago. We should therefore attempt to examine more
closely the possibilities of actuality in those incidents Guerard
claims to be beyond our acceptance. Conrad seems to be thinking

---

[9]   Guerard, p. 32.
[10]   Howard Hartman, *The Seas Were Mine* (London, George G. Harrap
and Company, Ltd., 1936). The best treatment of the actual Jim is in
Norman Sherry's fascinating *Conrad's Eastern World* (London, Cambridge
Univ. Press, 1966).

of such doubting men when Marlow addresses some of his listeners:

"Absurd!" he cried. "This is the worst of trying to tell. . . . Here you all are, each moored with two good addresses, like a hulk with two anchors, a butcher round one corner, a policeman round another, excellent appetites, and temperature normal – you hear – normal from year's end to year's end. And you say, Absurd! Absurd be exploded! Absurd! [11]

Any reader does well to consciously realize when approaching Conrad's fiction that, as highly symbolic as it often is, one must not lose touch with actuality merely because Conrad's actuality often appears fantastic. In reverse, knowing the actuality of his fantastic also enables the reader to be aware of the symbolic use Conrad makes of what at first sight appears to be ordinary and factual.

[11] *Heart of Darkness*, in *Youth*, p. 114.

I

THE WHITE MAN'S BURDEN:
"KARAIN: A MEMORY" AS A SYMBOLIC
STATEMENT OF THE BURDEN ASSUMED ▲

It is difficult to disentangle the conception of the white man's burden from the conceptions of "empire" and "colonization". The two writers in the English language who have in recent times concerned themselves in a major body of work with this subject are Conrad and Kipling. William York Tindall makes the distinction between two of the above concepts when he writes of Conrad's "producing many novels and stories that without being imperialistic are colonial".[1] However, in a recent discussion of the two terms in question, Professor William Berger, historian and political scientist, pointed out that the modern historian's connotation of colonialism tends to be one of a close tie with a controlling formal home government, whereas "empire" is no longer tightly or even necessarily associated with governmental overlordship. Conrad's concept is far more closely related to the late Latin Empire *colonus*, the man more on his own on the border of foreign regions than under the government and protection of a strong central political power. Such a concept allows Conrad to examine and see his characters as individuals, independent as much as possible of governmental ties, exposed to a greater power, Fate, against which they can match their intrinsic worths in areas not their own.

Professor Donald Davidson remarked in conversation that Conrad treated on a more elevated plane the same subject which

---

[1] *Forces in Modern British Literature 1885-1956*, p. 59.

occupies much of Kipling's literary consideration. This is a convenient starting point since it permits utilization of a general comparison. Conrad's treatment of the colonial *milieu* is not only on a more elevated plane, but is on a far broader one. Whereas Kipling deals with the East in terms of the "burden" in British areas, Conrad deals with the relation of the British with the East in other European areas of control as well as in their own spheres of influence. In so doing, he has as secondary consideration, observations to make on the intercourse of the Orient with French, Spanish, Portugese, and Dutch nationals. He also deals with the ethical and cosmic aspects of the subject by the use of the most involved symbolism. Kipling keeps his treatment mainly at the levels of military and material Empire.

Conrad directly commits himself in two books of essays, *The Mirror of the Sea* and *Notes on Life and Letters*. In the first he has a section entitled "The Weight of the Burden",[2] in which on the surface he discusses the arrangement of cargo in the storage holds of ships. From his language we are able to surmise that he is writing about far more than physical weight of trade goods. Discussing the trying conditions of preparing one ship, he notes that "it would have taken much more than this to extinguish my sacred fire for the exercise of my craft".[3] His sacramental attitude toward man's involvement in the weight of the burden is further brought out in:

Ships do want humouring. They want humouring in handling; and if you mean to handle them well, they must have been humoured in the distribution of the weight which you ask them to carry through the good and evil fortunes of a passage. Your ship ... must be attended to if you mean her to come with credit to herself and you through the rough-and-tumble of her life.[4]

The sacramental attitude and the "burden" are both more explicitly defined in *Notes on Life and Letters*. He claims that adventure, quite often thought of as "the second nature of British

---

² Pp. 45-56.
³ *Ibid.*, p. 50.
⁴ *Ibid.*, pp. 51-52.

men", is not as an important component of the "burden" as is the responsibility of service:

I venture to affirm that the main characteristic of the British men spread all over the world, is not the spirit of adventure so much as the spirit of service. I think that this could be demonstrated from the history of great voyages and the general activity of the race. ...

The mere love of adventure is no saving grace. It is no grace at all. It lays a man under no obligation of faithfulness to an idea and even to his own self. ... Yes, there is nothing more futile than an adventurer, but nobody can say that the adventurous activities of the British race are stamped with the futility of a chase after mere emotions.

The successive generations that went to sea from these Isles went out to toil desparately in adventurous conditions. A man is a worker. If he is not that he is nothing. Just nothing – like a mere adventurer. Those men understood the nature of their work, but more or less dimly, in various degrees of imperfection.[5]

It is that last sentence which lends maturity and humanism to the passage.

In his fiction, Conrad, through Marlow, comes to the heart of the matter: "What redeems it is the idea only. An idea at the back of it; not a sentimental pretense but an idea; and an unselfish belief in the idea – something you can set up, and bow down before, and offer a sacrifice to. ..." [6] The sacramental – and sacrificial, as we shall see in the consideration of other books – tone is maintained as Marlow observes the Thames: ". . . they all had gone out on that stream, bearing the sword, and often the torch, messengers of the might within the land, bearers of a spark from the sacred fire. What greatness had not floated on the ebb of that river into the mystery of an unknown world." [7] Conrad never loses touch in his Eastern fiction with the above interpretation of the "idea". In fact, as will be apparent from the numerous quotations in this study, he never loses touch with the term itself. As he sees it, such an "idea" in history has been limited to the Anglo-Saxons. The other great colonizers – the Portugese, the Dutch, the Spanish, and the French, even the Romans – could not be said to espouse such an "idea", so that

---

[5]   Pp. 189-190.
[6]   *Heart of Darkness*, p. 51.
[7]   *Ibid.*, p. 47.

the sense of white man's burden has been in origin and practice,
English. Marlow, speaking for that nation, claims:

What saves us is efficiency – the devotion to efficiency. But these
chaps [Romans, signifying the other nations] were not much account,
really. They were no colonists; their administration was merely a
squeeze, and nothing more, I suspect. They were conquerors, and for
that you want only brute force – nothing to boast of, when you have
it, since your strength is just an accident arising from the weakness
of others. They grabbed what they could get for the sake of what was
to be got. It was just robbery with violence, aggravated murder on a
great scale, and men going at it blind – as is very proper for those
who tackle a darkness. The conquest of the earth, which mostly means
the taking it away from those who have a different complexion or
slightly flatter noses than ourselves is not a pretty thing when you
look into it too much.[8]

To repeat: "What redeems it is the idea only." If it were not for
this, we could take exception to Marlow's using the term "efficiency". The Germans, in a sense, were more efficient as Empire
builders than the English. The Teutonic mind tends to be doctri-
naire, meticulously working out programs which operate efficiently – on paper – and then rather ruthlessly ramming the programs
as much as possible into practice. In the Orient, maybe partly as
the result of frustration, maybe partly as the result of temperament, the Germans, by a somewhat malicious brutality, enforced
efficiency on peoples who neither understood nor worshipped it.
The English have been far more prone to observe the operation
of their colonial cultures and derive their approaches from what
they have seen, then draw up their program from that, thereby
coming out with more nearly matching "paper" and "practice"
than their German kin.

Even more efficient than the Germans were the Spanish, if we
consider efficiency in their own terms – that is to say, stripping
the colonies of their wealth to send to the mother country, which
was never satiated and always hungry. Their cruelty, though
extreme, was not always malicious, merely expedient. If one
could get more out of a slave by torturings and beatings, then

---

[8]   *Ibid.*, pp. 50-51.

torture and beat, even if he did die; there were always more. Admittedly this is not profitable for long range projects, but the Spanish project was not long range.[9]

The consideration of white man's burden as the major philosophy in Conrad's colonialism must revert to "idea", and for that reason no more definition of it will be attempted here; but it is hoped finally to leave the reader with a concept of what the burden is by Conrad's treatment of it. The long quotation above from *Heart of Darkness* demonstrates one of the deeper, and therefore more impressive, thought-provoking aspects of Conrad's consideration of the "burden", namely, his reluctance to accept it. But even though reluctant, his work indicates that the acceptance

[9]   In the mid-1930's, I spent many a Saturday afternoon looking out of my bedroom window on the second floor of our house in Manila, watching what seemed to be a weekly ceremony of the well-born and well-placed cultivated and courteous Spanish family whose house backed ours. They – there was always more than one member of the family present – would lead their Filipino houseboy out to the back compound of their house, tie him to a whipping post permanently set in the ground, and proceed to beat the living daylights out of him as he squalled and howled. It was not punitive in our sense, for when the Saturday ceremony was over, anger at no time having been shown, all would return quietly to the *casa*, including the momentarily noisy houseboy. It was done to insure the servant's efficiency for the coming week. Odd as this occurrence may seem, it was not an isolated situation. In many of the school yards of Manila there were still standing the whipping posts used for Filipino students when the Spanish allowed them to attend classes in the formerly Spanish operated schools. The Filipino students were required to recite on their knees, and it was "out to the whipping post" if they missed a question. Again, it was not vindictive maliciousness which promulgated such a system. As it was explained to me, the Spanish merely wished to impress on the "lowly" Filipinos that they should take full advantage of and appreciate the opportunity for education offered them by the Spanish government.

As in the case of Mr. A. of Ceylon, the physical beating does not seem to be the most amazing ingredient of the situation. One of the problems with Filipino servants during the time I lived in the Philippine Islands was their propensity to leave without notice an American family paying them thirty pesos a month, in order to take advantage of a chance to work in a Spanish household which would pay them five pesos a month and treat them like dogs. The servants' attitudes were that the Spanish represented "real masters", even though the Spanish government no longer controlled the Islands. It is this *milieu* of totally different values one must remember in reading colonial fiction to understand all the complexities of the relationship between the various Western minds with the various Eastern minds.

is a responsibility his heroes cannot ethically and justifiably reject: they must assume it.

In a brilliant piece of literary artistry, "Karain: A Memory", Conrad states practically the whole subject. The story is so complex and intricate in thought that it seems almost questionable to outline it. However to do so will assist in discussing it.

Three gun-runners – the captain being the unnamed narrator; Hollis, a young man; and Jackson – are trading guns with Karain, a rajah and warrior. Before becoming chief of his present followers Karain was a nobleman from Mindanao. The setting of the story takes place in that area of the East which was then under Spanish control. The narrator notes with what awe and adoration Karain's people respect him, describing the omnipotent attitude and stage-like though none the less genuine dignity of the Rajah – a trait typical of the East. There is fine description of the gold cloth, gold head-dresses, and bejeweled fingers and swords of the court which accompanies Karain when he makes his visits to the ship. At all times at his back stands, or sits, the old seer and sword-bearer, the only one who shows a seeming indifference to the regal presence. The court calls occur during the day. At night Karain comes aboard accompanied only by the ever-present sword-bearer. For these visits he is dressed in plain white and is without the richness of his day attire. Now is the time that the three officers and the Rajah converse in friendly and relaxed fashion. Karain always inquires first after the health of Queen Victoria, whose person and power have captured his imagination. During these times he will now and again reach behind him to make sure that the old man with the sword is there. Now and again he will cast a quick glance over his shoulder and then the old man will whisper something in his ear.

All goes well and the ship leaves to return with another load of rifles and powder. They look forward to seeing Karain because they as well as he have respect for each other and have enjoyed the informal visits at night when the court is absent. As a token of their esteem, the officers have brought a brass cannon as a gift to the Rajah. They are surprised when he does not come aboard to greet them, although the court appears with pay for the

shipment of arms. They learn that the old seer has died and that
Karain has shut himself up in his house and has not been seen
since. Night comes and still no visit, a fact which perplexes the
traders. All at once Karain's dripping figure strides into the room,
looking over his shoulder as he comes. He is in a terrible condition
of anxiety and fatigue from lack of sleep, from the long swim
from shore, and from an obvious deficiency of food. He finally
gains his breath after being assured there is no danger, and tells
his story.

When Karain's brother was the Ruler, his councillor and ad-
viser Pata Matara was a great friend and comrade in arms to
Karain. Local wars were fought until the Dutch, who had been
waiting until the factions had exhausted themselves, stepped in
with the offer to establish peace and engage in trade. No one had
an alternative to accepting the Dutch terms. All went well until
Matara's sister, a ravishingly beautiful and wilful lady, ran away
from her campong to live in the house of the red-haired Dutch
trader. Both she and the Dutchman ignored the demands of
Matara that she return or be returned to erase her disgrace. The
Dutchman leaves and takes Matara's sister with him. Matara
swears that the stain will be removed from his family by the death
of his sister at his own hands. He begins his search for them
with Karain as companion. After many years of travel, hardships,
and degradation (during which time the sister's image becomes an
illusion and ideal to Karain, talking to him at night by the fire,
consoling him, swimming in the sea after him, his constant companion, belonging only to him) they discover their victims. Matara
makes arrangements to run *amok* and kill his sister with a knife;
Karain, hiding in the bushes is to fire the rifle immediately afterwards and kill the Dutchman. Honor will then be saved. In his
heart of hearts Karain has vowed to save the sister. Before he
knows fully what he does, he shoots and kills Matara, his brother
in arms and purpose, when he rushes toward his sister as she sits
in her garden counting the pearls given her over the years by the
Dutchman.

Ever since then the wraith of his comrade has pursued him,
muttering, "Kill, Kill, Kill." Only the old man has the power to

keep off this nameless dread. Now the swordsman is dead and the apparition can pursue him. He must have help from the white men. They are puzzled as to what to do, realizing that they cannot do nothing. Hollis finally makes a talisman of a jubilee gilded sixpence and the ribbon and glove of his past loves. He then convinces Karain of its power and hangs it on his neck. The charm works and the Rajah's fears are removed. He goes ashore to his rejoicing people.

That presentation is deceivingly simple. The story is an out-spokenly conscious creation of symbolism. It is as artistic as it can be made, the epitome of Conrad's productions about which Guerard writes, "This symbolism must be achieved, however, without loss of the artist's automony, without [and here he quotes Conrad] 'surrender ... to occult and irresponsible powers'." [10] Conrad tells his reader – without stating, "Reader, this is a fairy tale" – that the story is not true in all its factual formation. Years after the event, Jackson, a minor character, remarks to the captain whom he has met in London:

"Do you know, I sometimes think that ———."

I stood still and looked at him

"Yes ... I mean, whether the thing was so, you know ... whether it really happened to him. ... What do you think?"

"My dear chap", I cried, "you have been too long away from home. What a question to ask! Only look at all this." [11]

They both look at the milling, teeming London street life about them. Jackson meditatively answers, "Ye-e-e-s." He says this one word again before he says it the third time: " 'Yes, I see it', said Jackson, slowly. 'It is there; it pants, it runs, it rolls; it is strong and alive; it would smash you if you didn't look out; but I'll be hanged if it is yet as real to me as ... the other thing ... say, Karain's story.' " [12]

Jackson had been away a long time, and Jackson knew the East, and he knew that it would be unlikely that a Moro (Karain was a Moslem and came from Mindanao) could in a few years have been a deck hand, servant, agricultural cooly, rattan cutter,

[10]   Guerard, p. 14.
[11]   "Karain: A Memory", p. 54.
[12]   *Ibid.*, p. 55.

pearl diver, and the many other things he relates having been on his, as Conrad writes, "obscure Odyssey of revenge".[13] In one job alone, that of pearl diving, it is almost essential to be born and reared. To anyone who knows Conrad's Eastern background he has openly declared himself. To those who are not familiar with the Orient he gives a broad hint. As Karain leaves, standing proudly and assuredly in his boat, raising both arms in salute and pointing to the charm, the three officers cheer him, impressing and puzzling the Rajah's Malays. It is at this point where, as the narrator, Conrad breaks out in a completely unrelated direct address to the reader, "I wonder what they thought; what he thought; . . . what the reader thinks?" [14]

I should like to suggest an interpretation of the story in Conrad's terms. One quality in Conrad which engenders deep respect is his constant awareness, whether it be conscious or unconscious, of the identity of the peoples about whom he writes. No matter what the relationship, he never thoughtlessly neglects or impugns whatever dignity may belong to the individuals involved; his treatment is the highest form of recognizing differences and values. He can draw the reader's attention to this quality by smooth and unobstrusive methods. The captain, in narrating the story and in telling about the nightly visits of the Rajah to the ship, drops the information: ". . . we treated him in a free and easy manner, which just stopped short of slapping him on the back, for there are liberties one must not take with a Malay. He said himself that on such occasions he was only a private gentleman coming to see other gentlemen whom he supposed as well born as himself." [15]

We have here a picture of congenial familiarity which breeds no contempt, presented in a relaxed style. But the reader is later on brought to a jolting halt and forced to look directly at this insistence of Conrad that identity be respected. When Karain comes rushing into the cabin, knife in hand, obviously terrorized and almost in a state of collapse, he gasps out something between

13   *Ibid.*, p. 40.
14   *Ibid.*, p. 52.
15   *Ibid.*, p. 12.

heaving breaths. And what are his first words? An apology for coming into his friends' presence bearing arms, whereupon he places the weapon upon the table within reach of all.[16] He then relates his story, in the beginning informing them,

> I swam off to you, with my kriss between my teeth. I, armed, I fled before a breath – to you. ... The wise old man has died, and with him is gone the power of his words and charms. And I can tell no one. No one. There is no one here faithful enough and wise enough to know. It is only near you, unbelievers, that my trouble fades like a mist under the eye of day.[17]

In both of the above cases, as well as in those which later will be pointed out in his other works, Conrad indicates that the respect people of different blood have for each other can exist when each remains true to his intrinsic self. Only by each one keeping for himself his own convictions, his own ways, his own responsibilities can the same plane of understanding be approached; only by realizing that each must do this can an equal level of ethical, intellectual, and moral appreciation, in that word's broadest meaning, be genuinely sought. It may never be completely attained but it can be approached, if the Anglo-Saxon remains such and the Oriental remains Orthodox in the basic issues of his philosophy. This is what Karain means when he says "unbelievers". He neither rejects from himself his beliefs, nor repudiates for them their ways. This is why he can tell of his broken taboos to them, "unbelievers", and cannot to his own devoted people.

Conrad in this same scene very artistically modifies an unrelenting identity so that it does not become a senseless ironbound vice. He indicates the courtesy in mixed communities of relaxing one's decorum in the little and non-essential ways of life. When Karain enters the cabin, wet with sea and rain, Hollis says, "Give him a dry sarong – give him mine; it's hanging up in the bathroom." [18] This striking symbol escapes people who live in societies where the men and women are allowed the privilege of wearing

16 *Ibid.*, p. 22.
17 *Ibid.*, p. 25.
18 *Ibid.*, p. 22.

almost anything – and usually do. In the East, a man's costume is more than just clothes; it signifies to others who he is – his caste, his religion; and it is respected as such. The revulsion created in the residents, both European and national, of the Eastern countries at the sight of some vulgar tourist parading the streets wearing a fez – a hat generally signifying the wearer to be of the Mohammedan faith – is comparable to the feeling a strong Catholic community would have if they should see some young woman strutting down an avenue with a bishop's stole flung jauntily across her shoulders.

Throughout the Far East, Middle East, and parts of Africa, a man in a sarong is a Mohammedan. Yet this is the garment the Anglo-Saxon has adopted, in some cases, for his own use – and that *only* in the privacy of his home. This article of attire reaches from the waist to the heel, is cool, comfortable, and decorous; therefore it is admirably suitable as a sleeping garment, the only use to which the white man puts it. Clothes among social equals of different groups in the East are rarely if ever exchanged. Conrad could not have been more specific in indicating that, while standing firm on the main matters of one's background, the individual must, in a realistic approach to life with others, be malleable when the situation warrants it with regard to minor conventions. This is the discretion and good taste of the "burden" generally respected.

It is hoped that enough evidence has been presented to show how extremely symbolic the story is, since the phantasy atmosphere becomes more and more pronounced as the tale proceeds. Conrad very early begins to develop the impression that Karain is not only a single man, not only a Malay rajah who finds relief from the demanding and constricting system of his Oriental rulership in the conversation and companionship of the white traders. "It was only on board the schooner, when surrounded by white faces, by unfamiliar sights and sounds, that Karain seemed to forget the strange obsessions that wound like a black thread through the gorgeous pomp of his public life." [19] There is no doubt that the Ruler found the gunrunners impressive: "to the last he

[19]   *Ibid.*, p. 12.

believed us to be emissaries of Government, darkly official persons furthering by our illegal traffic some dark scheme of high state-craft. Our denials and protestations were unavailing." [20] Karain is the whole East in his genuine concern, awe, and affection for Queen Victoria. Even today, among great masses of the inhabitants of that part of the world, the British reputation is high; in some areas, parts of India for example, it is higher than it has ever been before, since those people now see what justice and administration they suffer under their own rulers.

In this admiration for the British rule, Conrad makes his handling of the matter a deliberate device. The setting of the story, as indicated, is in the Philippine Archipelago at the time of Spanish control, which ended with the Spanish-American War of 1898. It is important to remember the fact that this area was not a major interest of British colonization or British control. Therefore Karain's preoccupation with English rule is as obvious a conscious injection of the Anglo-Saxon element as is the Rajah's turning to English traders when he could have more easily gone to the Spanish or Dutch in the area. In Conrad's works, if we are not actually told the nationality of the heroes and the villains, one has only to look at their names. Among the villains are Willems,[21] Kurtz,[22] Heemskirk,[23] Ricardo,[24] Schomberg,[25] the Frenchman,[26] and Niclaus.[27] The failures include Heyst,[28] Almayer,[29] Bamtz,[30] Renouard,[31] Jorgenson,[32] Corlier,[33] and Kayerts.[34] Some of the successes in one or more aspects of the

[20] *Idem.*
[21] *An Outcast of the Islands.*
[22] *Heart of Darkness.*
[23] "Freya of the Seven Isles", in *'Twixt Land and Sea.*
[24] *Victory.*
[25] *Ibid.*
[26] "Because of the Dollars", in *Within the Tides.*
[27] *Ibid.*
[28] *Victory.*
[29] *Almayer's Folly.*
[30] "Because of the Dollars".
[31] "The Planter of Malata", in *Within the Tides.*
[32] *The Rescue.*
[33] "An Outpost of Progress", in *Tales of Unrest.*
[34] *Ibid.*

"burden" are Jim,[35] Morrison,[36] Lingard,[37] Gould,[38] Davidson,[39] Hollis,[40] Marlow,[41] Captain Allistoun,[42] and MacWhirr.[43] All of the last mentioned are British.

Karain's insatiable curiousity about the Queen leads the three officers to concoct details. This they do in a sense of duty, a sense of responsibility which makes the details accommodate the "resplendent ideal" [44] of the Queen held by the Rajah. There is no compulsion in the business relationship of these men which drives the whites to maintain Karain's conception. The only compulsion lies in their sense of the "idea" in the "burden". Hollis voices this when he presents the charm. He is talking to the captain and to Jackson:

> She [Victoria] commands a spirit too – the spirit of her nation; a masterful, conscientous, unscrupulous, unconquerable devil ... that does a lot of good – incidentally ... a lot of good ... at times – and wouldn't stand any fuss from the best ghost out for such a little thing as our friend's shot. ... Help me to make him believe – everything's in that.[45]

Like Hollis, Lord Jim, who also carries the conviction of the "burden", recognizes that the belief in the "idea" can be a salvation for all men, and that part of the belief of the "idea" lies in proselytizing it, no matter what energy might be required. "When he got his idea he had to drive it into reluctant minds, through the bulwarks of fear, of selfishness. He drove it in at last." [46]

The undertone of reluctance is also expressed in the passage indicating a more shoddy attribute of the English – making profitable what they cannot make better. In the beginning, after unsuccessfully trying to dissuade Karain from carrying out a war

[35]   *Lord Jim.*
[36]   *Victory.*
[37]   *The Rescue, Almayer's Folly, An Outcast of the Islands.*
[38]   *Nostromo: A Tale of the Seaboard.*
[39]   *Victory* and "Because of the Dollars".
[40]   "Karain: A Memory", in *Tales of Unrest.*
[41]   *Heart of Darkness.*
[42]   *The Nigger of the Narcissus.*
[43]   *Typhoon,* in *Typhoon and Other Stories.*
[44]   "Karain: A Memory", p. 13.
[45]   *Ibid.*, pp. 49-50.
[46]   *Lord Jim*, p. 261.

of revolt, all the traders "could do for him was to see to it that the powder was good for the money and the rifles serviceable, if old".[47]

Two years of trading pass before Karain suddenly appears wet and terrorized. He is the East, a fugitive from its known fears turning for aid, guidance, justice, to the white man, which it has done for many, many decades. The Rajah turns to those whom he does not fully understand; he turns to them even so, since he feels from the depths of his being that he can say with assurance a few minutes after he reaches their presence, "All right, now." [48]

The old seer had died. The old sword-bearer – symbolic of that great detachment, that overpowering objectivity which is, and was, for the Rajah (the East) the only power of the Orient able to protect him from the avenging spirits of his broken taboos – the old sword-bearer was the one person who had remained unaffected, almost unconscious of the pomp and ceremony of Karain's court (his temporal surroundings). That old man for this Rajah is dead. Karain was appealing "to the strong life of white men. . . . He stretched out his arms as if to embrace it. . . ." [49] And what had he done to be pursued by demon spirits? He had aspired for something outside the Oriental system and his life. Matara's sister is never named in the story because she, who had become a dream, an illusion, is that vaporish and indefinable longing by the East for some concept better than what it has. The cold and inhuman practice of the Orient is at one and the same time in agreement with the removed objectivity of the resigned truth carved on the fabled emerald, "And this too, shall also pass away", and is at one and the same time in conflict with the high yearning mysticism contained in its magnificent philosophies. The complexity of these ethnic frustrations is even more awesome when we realize that the Oriental societies containing such turbulence of practice and principle have a longevity and continuum unexperienced in Western cultures. Karain vowed she would live, that he would save her. The aspiration is allowed by the system,

[47]   *Ibid.*, p. 19.
[48]   *Ibid.*, p. 23.
[49]   *Ibid.*, p. 26.

but not the overt attempt to realize it. In attempting to attain his reach he shattered the wall of restriction which defines the life of the East. He shot, and destroyed, his sworn companion, a manifestation of honor – his purpose. He fatally broke taboo. The aspiration was not realized. The demon was upon him.

Toward the end of his story, Karain shows how close he is to the breaking point.

For the first time that night a sudden convulsion of madness and rage passed over his face. His wavering glances darted here and there like scared birds in a thunderstorm. He jumped up shouting –

"By the spirits that drink blood: by the spirits that cry in the night: by all the spirits of fury, misfortune, and death, I swear – some day I will strike into every heart I meet – I . . ."

He looked so dangerous that we all three leaped to our feet. . . .[50]

Hollis's action is symbolic of the fact that not only did Karain, the East, need the "protection" of the "strong life of white men", but some form of control as well. With one sweeping gesture he sent the kriss clattering from the table. Conrad's observation, "very little more pressing was needed to make him swerve over into the form of madness peculiar to his race",[51] is given added gravity when we consider that as recently as the turn of this century the U.S. Army .45 automatic pistol was developed for the purpose of stopping these warriors, since no other fire-arm could immediately bring them down, even when often they were shot through the heart. As late as the mid 1930's I can remember the great respect and fear the other Philippino peoples showed to these proud Moros from Mindanao when they appeared on the streets of even such as large a city as Manila.

Within a minute Karain was calm and the kriss was handed to him as a sign of confidence. He thrust the knife into his sarong "with punctilious care to give his weapon a pacific position".[52]

The heavy guilt having worn away the power of Oriental detachment, Karain, looking for respite from his breaking the philosophy of his own people, says to the traders, "You know us . . . you understand our sorrows and our thoughts – our desires

---

[50] *Ibid.*, p. 43.
[51] *Ibid.*, p. 45.
[52] *Ibid.*, p. 43.

and our fears." [53] He then utters that final cry which cannot be ignored by those possessed of the "idea", "Give me your protection!" [54]

Many a time, as late as three and four years after India's independence, a white man travelling up-country or out-station would be surrounded by villagers, peons, and coolies salaaming and imploring, "When will the Sahibs come back; when will the Sahibs return?"

Because that somber riddle and that impassioned request has, through Conrad's masterfulness, been offered at all times with powerful dignity, the captain can well say, "We did not know what to do with that problem from the outer darkness. We three white men, looking at that Malay, could not find one word to the purpose amongst us – if indeed there existed a word that could solve that problem. We pondered, and our hearts sank." [55] The "burden" is not an easy one. Young Hollis, overcome and confused by something he cannot apparently control, says hopelessly, "By Jove, he seems to have a great idea of our power." [56] But Hollis realizes that he must find a solution, since "We can't, so to speak, turn our backs on his confidence and belief in us." [57] He avoids that atrophy of courage active in assuming responsibility, which is, perhaps just as destructive as is atrophy of muscle, bone, and nerve. Hollis's solution consists in a fabrication of more "details", but for a far more profound purpose than to perpetuate a high conception of Queen Victoria. He is dealing with the very existence of Karain, the Orient, who is threatening to abandon his people.

With monumental irony, Conrad composes the "charm" of leather from a slim white glove and a piece of ribbon – trifles of women who have in the past haunted Hollis's memory, but whom he has now rejected, as Karain finally rejected Matara's sister – and a Jubilee gilt sixpence with the likeness of the Queen impressed upon it, worth about eighteen cents. Hollis solemnly holds

[53] *Ibid.*, p. 44.
[54] *Ibid.*, p. 45.
[55] *Idem.*
[56] *Idem.*
[57] *Ibid.*, p. 47.

up the sixpence and proclaims it "the most powerful thing the white men know".[58] The term "unbelievers" now assumes a rather gross interpretation which Conrad will not, in his reluctance, let us forget.

But the charm works, because the material contribution being less than nothing, the ethical quality is that much more magnificent. Hollis, man of the "idea", has offered guidance through his active courage of conviction.

[58]   *Ibid.*, p. 49.

II

"ONE OF US"

The phrase "one of us" can include so wide a variety of men in Conrad's works that it becomes almost enigmatic in defining or limiting "us". Its broader inclusion takes in such concepts as merchant-adventurers, "face", the British, and the ethical qualities generally associated with manhood. These concepts are dealt with under their separate headings elsewhere in this study. But it is felt that "one of us" deserves a special examination since it obviously concerned Conrad consciously and unconsciously in relation to the man of "idea", his colonial. In *Lord Jim* alone, he uses the phrase a minimum of ten times.[1] That he is conscious of the phrase is indicated by the fact that he incloses it in quotation marks at least once in *Lord Jim*,[2] at least once in *Victory*,[3] and once italicizes the "us" of the phrase in *Lord Jim*.[4]

Even though a reader might justifiably conclude by attention to single instances of the use of "one of us", that "us" may be any men involved in the complexities of an awareness to life, an interpretation of the phrase based on Conrad's conglomerate use may produce a more thoroughly restricted picture of his heroes who bear the "burden". The characteristics of "us" can be rather well established by reference to the situations in which the phrase appears. First, Conrad admits that "perhaps, my Jim is not a type

[1] *Lord Jim*, pp. IX, 43, 78, 93, 106, 224, 325, 331, 361, 416.
[2] *Ibid.*, p. IX.
[3] *Victory*, p. 10.
[4] *Lord Jim*, p. 361.

of wide commonness". "Us" are therefore not the inclusive range
of humanity in general. Nor are "us" men outside the reality of
an actively engaged life, for Conrad is adamant that Jim, established as "one of us" before the story even begins, "is not a
product of coldly perverted thinking", and is "significant".[5] The
nationality of "us" is established in a passage following a long
tirade by the rascally captain of the *Patna* against the English, in
which he works himself up to "shpit" in a gesture against his
English "verflucte certificate" which has been taken away from
him for ignoble conduct as a sea captain. Marlow, in contrast,
shifts his view from the "patriotic Flensborg"[6] to Jim: "I liked
his appearance; I knew his appearance; he came from the right
place; he was one of us."[7] Jim comes from England.

The "us" are honest and dedicated, with a touch of romantic
altruism. We are given this in Jim's "frank aspect, . . . artless
smile, . . . youthful seriousness. He was of the right sort. He was
one of us."[8] Although not significant in their mere factualism in
involvement in life, "us" are "significant" in their actualism, their
altruistic representation of a dedication to an ideal, the "idea".
In Jim's case

> . . . [his] occasion was obscure, insignificant – what you will: a lost
> youngster, one in a million – but then [and this changes his entire
> importance] he was one of us; an incident as completely devoid of
> importance as the flooding of an ant-heap, and yet the mystery of his
> attitude got hold of [Marlow] as though he had been an individual in
> the forefront of his kind, as if the obscure truth involved were
> momentous enough to affect mankind's conception of itself. . . .[9]

And since "us" have in them this "obscure truth", they have it in
them to be "dangerous",[10] as any dedicated individuals potentially
are – as is Kurtz of *Heart of Darkness*, because he starts out as
"one of us" but lacks the strength of the "idea". Coupled with the
"obscure truth", the potential to be "dangerous", is the related

5   *Ibid.*, p. IX.
6   *Ibid.*, pp. 41-42.
7   *Ibid.*, p. 43.
8   *Ibid.*, p. 78.
9   *Ibid.*, p. 93.
10 *Ibid.*, p. 106.

quality of being "imaginative",[11] which makes the "us" even more unfathomable.[12]

Being "imaginative", the "us" are also vulnerable, which makes them aware of imperfection, as Marlow is aware when he says, "The truth can be wrung out of us only by some cruel, little, awful catastrophe." And yet being altruistic, "us" can maintain a hope and not succumb to abject pessimism. Marlow recognizes this in Jim, whose "ant heap little catastrophe" has "wrung out" his truth of imperfection, when he reports that Jim "could say he was satisfied . . . nearly"; and he can say this because "he is one of us".[13] Above all, the "us" are highly aware of honor, and proud in the best sense, as Jim indicates when he left the legend of sending "right and left at all those faces . . . [an] unflinching glance", as he falls "forward, dead . . . to go away from a living woman to celebrate his pitiless wedding with a shadowy ideal of conduct. . . . He is one of us. . . ." [14]

In another book, the independence of the "us" in actuality if not in fact, to serve the "idea" is reiterated in the subject of marriage. "Ours, as you remember, was a bachelor crowd; in spirit anyhow, if not absolutely in fact. There might have been a few wives in existence, but if so they were invisible, distant, never alluded to." [15] The colonial life is one of bachelorhood. Wives are gone on "home leave" for months at a time or seeing to the children's education in England. As late as the 1950's a great number of the English banks in the Orient had a stipulation that their employees, even at executive level, could not get married until after the first ten years in service. American firms followed suit, but insisted on bachelorhood for not so long a period of time. Executives were dismissed if they did not honor this stipulation of their contracts.

Morrison, also "one of us",[16] allows us to see more of the mundane characteristics of the "us". True, he is "not only honest

11   *Ibid.*, p. 224.
12   *Ibid.*, p. 331.
13   *Ibid.*, p. 325.
14   *Ibid.*, p. 416.
15   "Because of the Dollars", in *Within the Tides*, p. 175.
16   *Victory*, p. 10.

... [but] honourable, too",[17] and altruistic – too much so.[18] But
he adds the information that he is an "individual trader".[19] He
makes his living in commercial ventures as do the rest of "us".
Morrison, on a trip to London concerning his coal venture, loses
his place among the "us" by ceasing to be an exile, by leaving the
exciting and challenging East. "Nobody amongst us had any
interest in men who went home. They were all right; they did not
count any more. Going to Europe was nearly as final as going to
Heaven. It removed a man from the world of hazard and adventure." [20]

In the above, we can see the concept of "us" defined as a
clique of British, dedicated, honorable, humanistic, courageous
merchant-adventurers who bear the "burden". Following sections
of this study will deal in more detail with the relation of these men
with the peoples of colonial areas of the world. However, there is
one important point to be yet made in defining "us". This far, we
have seen the application of the phrase applied in a positive
sense; that is, a man or a quality is given as belonging to "us".
One of the most revealing passages in Conrad, which seals the
definition of "one of us", utilizes it in the negative of exclusion,
instead of the positiveness of inclusion. Many of the men in
Conrad's works have qualities found in "us", but do not belong.
In the one instance I could find of a character being described as
not included, the colonial philosophy is made clear.

Dain Waris, son of Doramin, is one of the most attractive and
sympathetic characters created by Conrad. He is in all respects,
"distinguished".

Of Dain Waris, his own people said with pride that he knew how to
fight like a white man. This was true; he had that sort of courage –
the courage in the open, I may say – but he had also a European
mind. [Conrad is using the term "European" here as it is used in the
Orient, to mean "white man's".] You meet them sometimes like that,
and are surprised to discover unexpectedly a familiar turn of thought,
an unobscured vision, a tenacity of purpose, a touch of altruism. ...

[17]   *Ibid.*, p. 18.
[18]   *Ibid.*, p. 10.
[19]   *Ibid.*, p. 24.
[20]   *Ibid.*, p. 23.

Dain Waris had a proud carriage, a polished, easy bearing, a temperament like a clear flame. His dusky face, with big black eyes, was in
action expressive, and in repose thoughtful. He was of a silent disposition; a firm glance, an ironic smile, a courteous deliberation of
manner seemed to hint at great reserves of intelligence and power.[21]

And what is most important to Conrad, he is, in the very best
sense, a true and devoted friend to Jim. But even so, Dain Waris
"had not Jim's racial prestige. . . . He was not the visible, tangible
incarnation of unfailing truth and of unfailing victory. Beloved,
trusted, and admired as he was, he was still one of *them*, while
Jim was one of *us*".[22] Revealingly enough, Conrad presents the
above short passage from the point of view of the natives, and
not from that of the Europeans.

---

[21] *Lord Jim*, pp. 261-262.
[22] *Ibid.*, p. 361.

III

KURTZ' INFIDELITY TO THE "IDEA"
OF THE BURDEN IN *HEART OF DARKNESS*

Whereas in "Karain: A Memory", Hollis is an admirable success, true to himself, true to his own people, and true to others turning to the white man, in *Heart of Darkness* Kurtz is in the furthest realm of the opposite direction: a failure, an ethical, material, and spiritual failure so foul, so abysmal, so depraved as to create awe, and thereby a false sense of magnificence. Kurtz is as intrinsically rotten as the putrid hippopotamus flesh the cannibals bring on board the river steamer commanded by Marlow. Out of "legitimate self-defence",[1] because of its nauseous stench, a great amount of the hippopotamus flesh is thrown overboard. Conrad alludes to the meat later in the story in context more direct than in its first appearance. We are again reminded of the "burden" and of a peculiarly British method of handling the less attractive aspects of it. The British themselves are aware of their propensity to pretend that situations, or even persons, do not exist by covering them up or ignoring them. (The Sepoy Revolt in India was a rather marked failure, among others, of the method to work successfully.)

The earth for us is a place to live in, where we must put up with sights, with sounds, with smells, too, by Jove! – breathe dead hippo, so to speak, and not be contaminated. And there, don't you see? your strength comes in, the faith in your ability for the digging of unostentatious holes to bury the stuff in – your power of devotion, not to yourself, but to an obscure, back-breaking business.[2]

[1] *Heart of Darkness*, p. 103.
[2] *Ibid.*, p. 117.

Kurtz' relation to the hippopotamus flesh is more apparent when we remember that the day after he died, "the pilgrims buried something in a muddy hole".[3]

If the thoughtful reader is not aware, the modern critic will assist him to become aware that *Heart of Darkness* contains themes of such magnitude and cosmic complexity that the story cannot be restricted to any narrow aspects of human life.[4] However, one of the themes, a concern of this study, is offered as Marlow, chatting with his cronies as they sit aboard a vessel moored in the Thames, contemplates the number of ships which had in the past left that waterway "bearing the sword, and often the torch, messengers of the might within the land, bearers of a spark from the sacred fire".[5] What follows is the depiction of the collapse of one man who, going out for the same reason as the "ships", but void of appreciation of the "idea", finally becomes governed by "a flabby, pretending, weak-eyed devil of a rapacious and pitiless folly".[6] (This "rapacious and pitiless folly" is also Conrad's judgment of the Belgian administration in their area of Africa, an overtone which dominates the whole story.)

Conrad, recognizing the differences of kind as well as degree, wrote of Africa and the Negroes as he never wrote of the Orient with its advanced cultures and civilization. Admittedly the terms "savage" and "primitive" appear time and time again with reference to the East, but always "to the east that harbours both light and darkness".[7] The term "light" is used throughout his works as a symbol for the higher range of enlightenment. Such interweaving and side-by-side existence of "light" and "darkness" prompts Conrad to say of the Islands, in a spirit of respect, "There are more spells than your commonplace magicians ever dreamed of." [8]

It is another matter with the Negro. There is no relaxing of his

[3]   *Ibid.*, p. 150.
[4]   Bruce Harkness, ed., *Conrad's "Heart of Darkness" and the Critics* (San Francisco, Wadsworth Publishing Company, Inc., 1960); Leonard F. Dean, ed., *Joseph Conrad's "Heart of Darkness": Backgrounds and Criticisms* (Englewood Cliffs, Prentice-Hall, Inc., 1960).
[5]   *Heart of Darkness*, p. 47.
[6]   *Ibid.*, p. 65.
[7]   "The Lagoon", in *Tales of Unrest*, p. 188.
[8]   *Victory*, pp. 6-7.

pessimism concerning this question and problem. In the introduction to *Nostromo*, he states that he is dealing with "Aristocracy and People, men and women, Latin and Anglo-Saxon, bandit and politician," [9] but throughout the entire book he displays an unrelenting contempt and repudiation of "Negro Liberals" [10] and those whose kinky hair indicates Negro blood.

In *Heart of Darkness* and *The Nigger of the Narcissus*, Conrad's attitude is stated more symbolically and profoundly. Marlow, penetrating up the river into Africa, could have imagined himself to have been "the first of men taking possession of an accursed inheritance, to be subdued at the cost of profound anguish and of excessive toil": [11] the first of people to assume the "burden" of these – not inhuman men – but men who "howled and leaped, and spun, and made horrid faces".[12] "They still belong to the beginning of time – had no inherited experience to teach them as it were." [13]

This deep primitiveness, this same unreformed savagery exists in James Wait, "nigger" of the *Narcissus*, under his correctly spoken English – the veneer of his contact with the white man. Conrad describes him as he first appears on the ship: "He held his head up in the glare of the lamp . . . a head powerful and misshapen with a tormented and flattened face – a face pathetic and brutal: the tragic, the mysterious, the repulsive mask of a nigger's soul." [14]

In this recognition of the vast difference between the Negro and other races and peoples lies an awareness which exists in all people who have first hand knowledge of the Negro in large numbers. In this country there is no doubt as to what the terms "colored" and "race" refer. We all know they have to do with the Negro. We have, out of an immature idea that we are being considerate by not using the word "Negro", projected these terms into circles and areas where the words mean what they state

9   *Nostromo: A Tale of the Seaboard*, p. xi.
10   *Ibid.*, p. 183.
11   *Heart of Darkness*, p. 95.
12   *Ibid.*, p. 96.
13   *Ibid.*, p. 103.
14   *The Nigger of the Narcissus*, p. 18.

– color, and race – but do not have in general the connotations we have given them. In Japan, China, India, Pakistan, Ceylon, and other Eastern countries there are peoples of different races and colors. In those countries there is now no color question – the term without quotation marks; and what racial problems exist are mostly ethnocentric, which are not only expected, but right and justified. These problems also have in almost every case a civilized solution which compromises no one. In those same countries, the Negro problem exists in that the people, in almost every instance, take the historical attitude toward the Negro in mass; in some of those countries, they assume a far less liberal attitude toward the "black man" than do the Occidental countries.

To administer and control the "accursed inheritance" one must have what?

Joy, fear, sorrow, devotion, valour, rage – who can tell? – but truth – truth stripped of its cloak of time. Let the fool gape and shudder – the man knows, and can look on without a wink. But he must at least be as much of a man as these on the shore. He must meet that truth with his own true stuff – with his own inborn strength. Principles won't do. Acquisitions, clothes, pretty rags – rags that would fly off at the first good shake. No; you want a deliberate belief.[15]

Identity, pride of respect, conviction – all in the positive!

In the beginning, Kurtz has a sense of the "idea". When he first arrives in Africa he expresses the belief that "each station should be like a beacon on the road towards better things, a centre for trade of course, but also for humanizing, improving, instructing". The Belgian company's comment on this approach comes out of the manager, "Conceive you – that ass!" [16] who then chokes with excessive indignation.

It was no unconscious act on Conrad's part that, having clearly differentiated between the Kurtz who first came to Africa and the abomination who died there, he relates the early Kurtz to his Anglo-Saxon heritage:

The original Kurtz had been educated partly in England, and – as he

[15] *Heart of Darkness*, pp. 96-97.
[16] *Ibid.*, p. 91.

was good enough to say himself – his sympathies were in the right place. His mother was half-English.[17]

This very casual and unobtrusive device in Conrad's works repeatedly relates the good qualities of even bad characters to some English connections or influence.

Further evidence of his sympathies' being in the right place appears in his report Marlow discovers, which was to have been sent back to Europe for publication in the journal of the "International Society for the Suppression of Savage Customs". In magnificent language Kurtz expounds the argument that because of our developments we "must necessarily appear to them [savages] in the nature of supernatural beings – we approach them with the might as of a diety. . . . By the simple exercise of our will we can exert a power for good practically unbounded. . . ." However, Kurtz reveals a horrifying method as his final judgment for the solution of the Negro problem in a note scrawled much later at the foot of the last page: "Exterminate all the brutes!" [18]

In the light of Kurtz' early expressions of purpose and his reputation for ability about which Marlow had heard much, it is no wonder that Marlow had been most anxious, exceedingly anxious, to meet this man. What he met was the antithesis of what he expected. Kurtz' collapse with regard to his own stated ideas was towering. The "power for good" which he exerted consisted of raiding the countryside with the help of a tribe of savages whom he used as a tool and weapon. He substituted for trade goods the use of cartridges in obtaining the ends [19] which developed after he gave up the high ideals of his report. "The wilderness", which is easily interpreted as the great challenge to Kurtz or any other man of intelligence or ambition, "had taken him, loved him, embraced him", and because he did not have it in him to see through to the "idea", "got into his veins, consumed his flesh, and sealed his soul to its own by the inconceivable ceremonies of some devilish initiation".[20] His foul desires "caused

[17]   *Ibid.*, p. 117.
[18]   *Ibid.*, p. 118.
[19]   *Ibid.*, p. 128.
[20]   *Ibid.*, p. 115.

him to preside at certain midnight dances ending with unspeakable rites, which – as far as I reluctantly gathered from what I heard at various times – were offered up to him".[21] They also awakened "brutal instincts, by the memory of gratified and monstrous passions". His inability to meet the challenge "had driven him out to the edge of the forest, to the brush, towards the gleam of fires, the throb of drums, the drone of weird incantations; this alone had beguiled his unlawful soul beyond the bounds of permitted aspirations".[22]

This depravity cannot be laid at the feet of the primitives who catered to him in his failure, for he was the "deity", he could have been the "power for good" if he had had the "will". His depravity does not stop with "gratified and monstrous passions". His egotistic selfishness was overwhelming. It appears in even greater contrast when we compare it to the selflessness of Jim, of the early Lingard, of Morrison, of Hollis, of the crew of the *Narcissus* toward James Wait. "You should have heard him say, 'My ivory.' Oh yes, I heard him. 'My Intended, my ivory, my station, my river, my –' everything belonged to him." [23] "I saw him open his mouth wide – it gave him a weirdly voracious aspect, as though he had wanted to swallow all the air, all the earth, all the men before him." [24] The last phrase is not merely figurative when we remember Kurtz is in cannibal country.

And what, in the concrete, was that gaping maw devouring as a dainty, as a desire? Conrad gives us an example of the barbaric savagery for which the civilized Kurtz had failed – a Negress:

She walked with measured steps, draped in striped and fringed cloths, treading the earth proudly, with a slight jingle and flash of barbarous ornaments. She carried her head high; her hair was done in the shape of a helmet; she had brass leggings to the knee, brass wire gauntlets to the elbow, a crimson spot on her tawny cheek, innumerable necklaces of glass beads on her neck; bizarre things, charms, gifts of witchmen, that hung about her, glittered and trembled at every step.[25]

[21] *Ibid.*, p. 118.
[22] *Ibid.*, p. 144.
[23] *Ibid.*, p. 116.
[24] *Ibid.*, p. 134.
[25] *Ibid.*, p. 135.

This passage is stronger as a symbol of the shoddy when we remember the care and delight Conrad takes in describing the gold, jewels, and magnificent fabrics of the native women in his Malay and other Eastern settings. Marlow comments earlier in the story on the poor quality of the trade "fringed-cloth". Princess Immada's gold brocade on silk is in marked contrast, as are the gold to the "brass", the gems to the "bizzare things". Aïssa is beautiful whereas this Negress is "savage and superb".[26] Matara's sister counts the magnificent pearls given her by the Dutchman; the Negress has "glass beads" and "charms" (dried animal parts, more than likely) given her by "witch-men".

No such base depths would be tolerated in Conrad's Eastern settings. The main characters could not be so elevated in power and wretched in morality. The situation of a main European character being in a comparable position of elevated power and moral degradation would not be tolerated by many native people of those places, who would reject or disallow such a man because of their own sense of ethnocentric ethics. The wretched European characters of Conrad's Indian and Malay settings occupy places of low esteem in the eyes of the native population. In this way we are made conscious of the Negro problem and its difference to the Race problem.

It has been shown how Kurtz failed the "blacks". He also fails his own people. On the way up the river to investigate what has happened to Kurtz, rumors of his illness having reached the company's main station, the river steamer with the Belgian officials and Marlow on board is attacked by savages. Marlow is the man who makes the startling discovery "that it was Kurtz who had ordered the attack to be made on the steamer".[27] He ordered it with the idea of frightening the steamer back, knowing, however, that possibly some whites as well as many of his "tribe" would be killed. This lack of concern is indirectly criticized, in that Marlow's sense of responsibility for his native helmsman, "a savage who was no more account than a grain of sand in a black

---

26   *Idem.*
27   *Ibid.*, p. 139.

Sahara",[28] is quite strongly stressed. "I had to look after him, I worried about his deficiencies, and thus a subtle bond had been created, of which I only became aware when it was suddenly broken." This unconscious assumption bespeaks a finer trait in Marlow than if all his care had been premeditated. "I missed my late helmsman awfully, – I missed him even while his body was still lying in the pilot-house." [29] Marlow had closed the shutter of the wheel house on the jungle side, but the "poor fool" [30] had opened it and been pierced by a spear. Marlow tosses him overboard during the running battle, determined that the "very second-rate helmsman" [31] would be eaten by the fishes instead of the cannibals on the steamer. They had been without their customary food for some time.

In this tangle of degradation, the aspect most condemning Kurtz is his cosmic irresponsibility in not realizing how untrue all of the "mine" is. "Everything belonged to him – but that was a trifle. The thing was to know what he belonged to. . . ." [32] No matter how awful was Kurtz' lack of intrinsic worth, there was not even diabolical dignity, since he was completely cut loose from any ideal or any principle. This in itself created a dangerous problem, for when Kurtz "escaped" from the river-boat and returned to the village, endangering the ship and all on board, Marlow, attempting to bring him back, was faced with the situation of dealing with a man to whom he "could not appeal in the name of anything high or low".[33]

If he makes a row we are lost, I thought to myself. This clearly was not a case for fisticuffs, even apart from the very natural aversion I had to beat that Shadow – this wandering and tormented thing. "You will be lost", I said – "utterly lost". One gets sometimes such a flash of inspiration, you know. I did say the right thing, though indeed he could not have been more irretrievably lost than he was at this very moment. . . . "I had immense plans", he muttered irresolutely. . . . "I

28 *Ibid.*, p. 119.
29 *Idem.*
30 *Idem.*
31 *Ibid.*, p. 120.
32 *Ibid.*, p. 116.
33 *Ibid.*, p. 144.

was on the threshold of great things", he pleaded, in a voice of longing, with a wistfulness of tone that made my blood run cold.[34]

It is no compliment to us that Kurtz could be told, "Your success in Europe is assured in any case",[35] that he could succeed in our civilization but not where he must be governed by the "idea". In the final analysis, his entire collapse is due to his being "hollow at the core",[36] without identity.

Marlow was unable to tell Kurtz' Intended his last words since "it would have been too dark – too dark altogether".[37] Expecting the heavens to fall on his head, he informs the young lady that Kurtz' last syllables were her name, instead of, as we know, an unconscious realization of himself – "the horror! the horror!" [38]

---

[34]   *Ibid.*, p. 143.
[35]   *Ibid.*, pp. 143-144.
[36]   *Ibid.*, p. 131.
[37]   *Ibid.*, p. 162.
[38]   *Ibid.*, p. 161.

IV

JAMES WAIT AS A SYMBOL OF THE BURDEN
IN *THE NIGGER OF THE NARCISSUS*

Since it is often difficult to determine what a writer says, consciously or unconsciously, if he is extremely symbolic, complex, or dealing in unfamiliar backgrounds, we are forced to expend some energy in meditating on his works. Conrad writes in *Victory*, "a meditation is always – in a white man, at least – more or less an interrogative exercise"; [1] as a result, we arrive at the question of what we should use for a basis of judging the conscious and unconscious intents of the author. In this paper, conscious and unconscious are based on knowledge of the author's background and the attitudes it engenders, what he has written elsewhere, and secondary information which supports the background and the writings.

Just as geographical Africa *per se* is not the theme of *Heart of Darkness*, but is used as a locale symbol for the very core of an "accursed inheritance", James Wait as an individual man is not the theme of *The Nigger of the Narcissus*, but is used as a symbol of the specific race who come from the heart of darkness. In this sense, Conrad's colonialism is in keeping with the climate of opinion of his time. From a removed and objective point of view, we can easily understand his traditional attitude toward the Negro when we realize that the Oriental area in which he moved has a history of slavery and of Negro slavery which precedes ours by literally thousands of years. The Japanese word for Negro translates into "beast". Tribes of South Pacific areas considered

[1] *Victory*, p. 173.

primative by the rest of the world look down on the Negro and label them "lizzard eaters", that dish being considered rather low. The present day practice of black Africans to eat their political opponents leaves something to be desired in the way of diplomatic conduct.

Near the beginning of *The Nigger of the Narcissus* we are given indication that James Wait is more than simply an "obnoxious nigger".[2] He represents the dependent peoples of the world (more specifically and more strongly the Negro problem, since its assumption results in, or is cursed with, the greater "anguish".) He is a disease, existing in powerful contrast to illness in Conrad's other works. Sickness is a political and personal pretense to the Rajah Lakamba. He resorts to it when a situation becomes too difficult for him to handle, or if he wants to gain time, or if he wants to save himself from personal discomfort. When Lakamba is told that the Dutch officials will come to his compound to question him about an illegal transaction in gunpowder in which he is involved, he has this to say: " 'Speak to the Rajah!' repeated Lakamba, thoughtfully. 'Listen, Babalatchi [his prime-minister]: I am sick, and shall withdraw; you cross over and tell the white men.' "[3] Babalatchi leaves to do the bidding, thinking, "He may be very sick for the white men, for all the world if he liked, as long as he would take upon himself the execution of part at least of Babalatchi's carefully thought-out plan."[4]

The same stratagem is practised by Colonel Sotillo, a South American in *Nostromo*. "A flash of craven inspiration suggested to him an expedient not unknown to European statesmen when they wish to delay a difficult negotiation. Booted and spurred, he scrambled into the hammock with undignified haste."[5] The poor man had contracted, all of a sudden, a severe fever!

This trick, known everywhere in the world, seems to be particularly prevalent in the Orient and in the South of the U.S.A. where "mis'ries" is a frequent excuse for irresponsibility. It is a

2   *The Nigger of the Narcissus*, p. 36.
3   *Almayer's Folly*, p. 130.
4   *Ibid.*, p. 131.
5   *Nostromo: A Tale of the Seaboard*, p. 442.

plea unusually powerful with the white man who does not have the Eastern attitude of working a person while he is sick. It is a term which will generate much consideration and kindness in the Anglo-Saxon. For these reasons, servants make full use of it.

As Ali, head servant to Almayer in *An Outcast of the Islands*, rushed about to arouse some workmen for their white master, some wanted time for food, some time to stretch, and "one said he was sick." [6] In *Victory*, the situation has become too much for Wang, Heyst's Chinese servant. He steals a revolver and then wants to leave his job. Accused of being frightened – " 'Me no flightened', protested Wang raucously, throwing up his head – which gave his throat a more strained, anxious appearance than ever. 'Me no likee', he added in a quieter tone. 'Me velly sick.' " [7] Heyst must answer as has answered every white man who has resided in the Orient when the limits of tolerance have been reached: " 'That', said Heyst, serenely positive, 'belong one piecee lie'." [8]

But it is profound and diabolical truth in the case of James Wait. Immediately after he comes on board, enunciating distinctly, "I belong to the ship", thereby not so much commending himself to the world's care as identifying himself as one of the cares of the world, he has an attack of sickness that is in no way feigned. "He put his hand to his side and coughed twice, a cough metallic, hollow, and tremendously loud; it resounded like two explosions in a vault; the dome of the sky rang to it, and the iron plates of the ship's bulwarks seemed to vibrate in unison." [9] It was an evil problem which wracked the world of that vessel.

In connection with the Negro situation in this country and in modern South Africa, Conrad's foresight is quite startling. This same profound foresight is displayed in *The Secret Agent* and day Europe swamped under Russian communism. The most *Under Western Eyes* [10] with regard to the situation of a present-

[6]   *An Outcast of the Islands*, p. 321.
[7]   *Victory*, p. 311.
[8]   *Ibid.*, p. 312.
[9]   *The Nigger of the Narcissus*, pp. 18-19.
[10]   Joseph Conrad, *The Secret Agent* (New York, Doubleday, Page and Company, 1921); Joseph Conrad, *Under Western Eyes* (New York, Harper and Brothers, 1911).

amazing example of such a critical ability occurs in *Nostromo* in the one sentence definition, in context, of our own contemporary U.S. foreign policy.

From the minute he put foot on board the *Narcissus*, "James Wait was disturbing the peace of the ship." [11] At first the crew were unable to detect the sickness, the problem, buried in the "nigger"; but soon "he became the tormentor of all our moments; he was worse than a nightmare. You couldn't see that there was anything wrong with him: a nigger does not show." He displayed that lack of responsibility and that erratic performance often complained of in the dependent peoples. When asked, after he states he is a "dying man", why, then, did he ship aboard, he answered,

"I must live till I die – mustn't I?" He coughed often, but the most prejudiced person could perceive that, mostly, he coughed when it suited his purpose. He wouldn't, or couldn't, do his work – and he wouldn't lie up. One day he would ship aloft with the best of them, and next time we would be obliged to risk our lives to get his limp body down.[12]

The crew took care of him, coddled him, and tended to all his needs. He, through his fear of truth – his coming death – denied it and attempted to assert his well being, his equality in life and living. Of course it could not work to treat him as an equal in the active life, or to attend to his needs in his passive force arising from the false attitude that he was equal.

He was demoralizing. Through him we were becoming highly humanized, tender, complex, excessively decadent: we understood the subtlety of his fear, sympathized with all his repulsions, shrinkings, evasions, delusions – as though we had been over-civilized, and rotten, and without any knowledge of the meaning of life. ... We were inexpressibly vile and very much pleased with ourselves. We lied to him with gravity, with emotion, with unction, as if performing some moral trick with a view to an eternal reward. We made a chorus of affirmation to his wildest assertions, as though he had been a millionaire, a politician, or a reformer – and we a crowd of ambitious lubbers. When we ventured to question his statements we did it after the manner of obsequious sycophants, to the end that his glory should

[11]   *The Nigger of the Narcissus*, p. 46.
[12]   *Ibid.*, p. 44.

be augmented by the flattery of our dissent. He influenced the moral tone of our world as though he had it in his power to distribute honours, treasures, or pain.[13]

And what could he give in return for this near-complete loss of all human dignity and identity, for all this misspent concern? Only that which has through all time been repaid by inferiors for such treatment – "he could give us nothing but his contempt." [14]

The contempt, however, does not deter Belfast, a member of the crew, from making a fetish of James Wait. As do so many people who become obsessed with the misconception of the Negro's equality, Belfast does lose all sense of proportion.

He spent every moment of his spare time in Jimmy's cabin. He tended him, talked to him; was as gentle as a woman, as tenderly gay as an old philanthropist, as sentimentally careful of his nigger as a model slave-owner. But outside he was irritable, explosive as gunpowder, sombre, suspicious, and never more brutal than when most sorrowful. With him it was a tear and a blow: a tear for Jimmy, a blow for any one who did not seem to take a scrupulously orthodox view of Jimmy's case.[15]

In turn, the "nigger" treats Belfast worse than anyone else. The only person he shows the slightest respect for is Donkin, a filthy, despicable, little unionizer and rabble rouser who torments and mistreats James Wait, who finally jeers at him as he goes into his death coma, and who then proceeds to steal the dead man's money.

However, as miserable as this burden was to the ship, officers, and crew, it had to be assumed. Ignoring the problem would have been as impossible as solving it by any method other than Kurtz' "Exterminate all the brutes!"

The very fact that Captain Allistoun has kept his sense of perspective amid all the warped attitudes toward James Wait

We could not scorn him safely – neither could we pity him without risk to our dignity. So we hated him, and passed him carefully from hand to hand. We cried, "Got him?" – "Yes. All right. Let go." And he swung from one enemy to another, showing about as much life as an old bolster would do.[16]

13   *Ibid.*, p. 139.
14   *Ibid.*, pp. 139-140.
15   *Ibid.*, p. 140.
16   *Ibid.*, p. 73.

leads to a near mutiny. A man usually aloof and removed from any sympathetic contact with the crew, he shows consideration for the sick "nigger" which he would not have shown to a white man.

When I saw him standing there, three parts dead and so scared – black amongst that gaping lot – no grit to face what's coming to us all – the notion came to me all at once, before I could think. Sorry for him – like you would be for a sick brute.[17]

The "notion" was to ease the fear of the "nigger" by pretending that he was not really ill. The Captain, therefore, accuses James Wait of malingering and restricts him to his cabin, a private cubby-hole fitted out by the crew for Wait's comfort. This appears to the crew a monstrous act of inhumanity, even though he has not come out of his quarters very often. They then work themselves into a mutinous mood. The captain, with his white attitude toward an inferior, thinks the crew understood his gesture to lessen Wait's fear. But we have seen how unbalanced their outlook had become.

James Wait has behaved throughout the book with the colonial concept of the characteristics of the "problem", lack of responsibility, lack of gratitude, lack of courage, and above all, lack of any effort to help himself. After the crew exhaust themselves and risk their lives to save him during a raging storm, in which he has not been hurt or forced to expend any energy even to assist in his own rescue,

He wouldn't stand; he wouldn't even as much as clutch at our necks; he was only a cold black skin loosely stuffed with soft cotton wool; his arms and legs swung jointless and pliable; his head rolled about; the lower lip hung down, enormous and heavy.[18]

As over the true heroics of his rescue, still

He overshadowed the ship. Invulnerable in his promise of speedy corruption he trampled on our self-respect, he demonstrated to us daily our want of moral courage; he tainted our lives. Had we been a miserable gang of wretched immortals, unhallowed alike by hope and fear, he could not have lorded it over us with a more pitiless assertion of his sublime privilege.[19]

[17]   *Ibid.*, p. 127.
[18]   *Ibid.*, p. 71.
[19]   *Ibid.*, p. 47.

James Wait is the same primitive challenge which victoriously engulfs Kurtz in *Heart of Darkness*.

In all of their degradation, the men keep a certain amount of dignity. They do not succumb completely. After the crew ease Wait into a comfortable position subsequent to his rescue,

he mumbled peevishly, "It took you some time to come. I began to think the whole smart lot of you had been washed overboard. What kept you back? Hey? Funk?" We said nothing. With sighs we started again to drag him up. The secret and ardent desire of our hearts was the desire to beat him viciously with out fists about the head; and we handled him as tenderly as though he had been made of glass.[20]

The men have not irretrievably lost hold of their superiority; they did not beat him.

The solution came at last with Wait's removal. Sewed in canvass and weighted with stone and steel, he was still reluctant to leave the ship. His body caught on a nail in the plank down which he was to have glided into the sea, and did not slip loose until Belfast shouted, "Go, Jimmy! – Jimmy, go!" As the faint circle of a vanishing ripple formed, "the ship rolled as if relieved of an unfair burden".[21]

Neither final solution even approaches satisfaction: death administered, according to Kurtz, nor death by nature. The one is as abhorrently degrading as the other is tedious in coming.

[20]   *Ibid.*, p. 73.
[21]   *Ibid.*, p. 160.

V

THE RELATION OF VARIOUS POSITIVE ASPECTS OF THE BURDEN TO BRITISH CHARACTERISTICS AND OF NEGATIVE ASPECTS TO NON-BRITISH CHARACTERS

Up to this point, the white man's burden as a major vehicle of Conrad's colonialism has been defined by three main works: *The Nigger of the Narcissus*, as the "burden" itself; "Karain: A Memory", as a depiction of the courage of responsibility necessary to assume the "burden"; and *Heart of Darkness*, as a contrast powerful enough in the negative to strongly stress the positive aspect. Each of these stories is so concisely complete that the three together form a convenient, if rather elaborate, introduction to the subject of this thesis. From this point on, it will be more convenient to discuss the various works of Conrad under the headings of different phases of the "burden".

There is no denying that Europeans in the Orient fully enjoy, as Conrad tells us the ship's officers who chose to stay in the East do enjoy, among other things, "the distinction of being white".[1] There is no denying, either, that there is a distinction in the Orient in being white. The Colonial British have had the advantage of being the last great white power in the East. They also have the credit for embodying the rules of life which increase the "distinction". Therefore, a strong predilection exists throughout the East, as well as other parts of the world, to link the attitudes "White" and "British". Even today, the remaining Colonial British, representing the older English stock, are a different breed from their socialistic-turned insular brothers.

Conrad calls attention to this British difference when com-

[1] *Lord Jim*, p. 13.

paring "Charles Gould, the Idealist-creator of Material Interests" and "Nostromo, the second of the two racially . . . contrasted men . . . captured by the silver of the San Tome Mine." About the latter, he writes: "Had he been an Anglo-Saxon he would have tried to get into local politics. But Nostromo does not aspire to be a leader in a personal game. He does not want to raise himself above the mass." [2] We must remember that "getting into politics" to Conrad did not necessarily have the same smutty aura that the phrase often exudes today. It definitely is the Anglo-Saxon nature to want to rise – as it is the Eastern nature to respect anything – "above the mass".

The reader is constantly kept in touch with Conrad's belief in the good quality of Anglo-Saxon traits by the author's continual injection of English identity into non-English situations and non-English people who, notwithstanding, portray admirable attributes. Karain turns to Englishmen in an area where the Dutch or the Spanish would have been not only more easily contacted, but the legal sources of aid. The early, undefiled Kurtz is closely related to his English background. Heyst, the Swedish Baron of *Victory*, was educated in England and conforms to some English customs. Both Almayer and Willems make a point of speaking English in a strictly Dutch area. Renouard, the hero of "The Planter of Malata", replies when asked if he is French, "I told her my people were living in Canada, but that I was brought up in England before coming out here." [3]

Of Dain Waris [native friend of Lord Jim], his own people said with pride that he knew how to fight like a white man. This was true; he had that sort of courage – the courage in the open, I may say – but he also had a European mind. You meet them sometimes like that, and are surprised to discover unexpectedly a familiar turn of thought, an unobscured vision, a tenacity of purpose, a touch of altruism.[4]

In a like manner, the traits of the Malays which Conrad admires can be applied, in part, to the English: "love of liberty, fanatical devotion to their chiefs, [and] their blind fidelity in friendship",

[2]   *Nostromo: A Tale of the Seaboard*, p. xii.
[3]   "The Planter of Malata", p. 10.
[4]   *Lord Jim*, pp. 261-262.

as well as the sea's being their home as much as the land.[5] "The immigrants from Celebes . . . are intelligent, enterprising, . . . with a more frank courage than the other Malays, and restless under oppression." [6]

Captain MacWhirr represents the essence of British stolidity. It was hardly necessary to talk, according to him, for "the past being to his mind done with, and the future not there yet, the more general actualities of the day required no comment – because facts can speak for themselves with overwhelming precision".[7] Conrad offers him to us with a benign and sympathetic, yet knowing, criticism of that quality of the British character. Jukes, his young chief mate, was much upset that their ship, the *Nan-Shan*, even though sold to a Siamese firm, was taken from under the British flag and placed under the Siamese national symbol.

She had come out on a British register, but after some time, Messrs. Sigg judged it expedient a transfer her to the Siamese flag.

At the news of the contemplated transfer Jukes grew restless, as if under a sense of personal affront. He went about grumbling to himself, and uttering short scornful laughs. "Fancy having a ridiculous Noah's Ark elephant in the ensign of one's ship", he said once at the engine-room door. "Dash me if I can stand it: I'll throw up the billet. Don't it make *you* sick, Mr. Rout?" The chief engineer only cleared his throat with the air of a man who knows the value of a good billet.

The first morning the new flag floated over the stern of the *Nan-Shan* Jukes stood looking at it bitterly from the bridge. He struggled with his feelings for awhile, and then remarked, "Queer flag for a man to sail under, sir."

"What's the matter with the flag?" inquired Captain MacWhirr. "Seems all right to me." And he walked across to the end of the bridge to have a good look.

"Well, it looks queer to me", burst out Jukes, greatly exasperated, and flung off the bridge.

Captain MacWhirr was amazed at these manners. After a while he stepped quietly into the chartroom, and opened his International Signal Code-book at the plate where the flags of all nations are correctly figured in gaudy rows. He ran his finger over them, and when he came to Siam he contemplated with great attention the red field and the

5   *The Rescue*, p. 3.
6   *Lord Jim*, p. 256.
7   *Typhoon*, p. 9.

white elephant. Nothing could be more simple; but to make sure he brought the book out on the bridge for the purpose of comparing the coloured drawing with the real thing at the flagstaff astern. When next Jukes, who was carrying on the duty that day with a sort of suppressed fierceness, happened on the bridge, his commander observed:

"There is nothing amiss with that flag."

"Isn't there?" mumbled Jukes, falling on his knees before a deck-locker and jerking therefrom viciously a spare lead-line.

"No. I looked up the book. Length twice the breadth and the elephant exactly in the middle. I thought the people ashore would know how to make the local flag. Stands to reason. You were wrong, Jukes. . . ."

"Well, sir", began Jukes, getting up excitedly, "All I can say – " He fumbled for the end of the coil of line with trembling hands.

"That's all right." Captain MacWhirr soothed him, sitting heavily on a little canvass folding-stool he greatly affected. "All you have to do is to take care they don't hoist the elephant upside-down before they get quite used to it."

Jukes flung the new lead-line over on the fore-deck with a loud "Here you are, bo'ss'en – don't forget to wet it thoroughly", and turned with immense resolution towards his commander; but Captain MacWhirr spread his elbows on the bridge-rail comfortably.

"Because it would be, I suppose, understood as a signal of distress," he went on. "What do you think? That elephant there, I take it, stands for something in the nature of the Union Jack in the flag. . . ."

"Does it!" yelled Jukes, so that every head on the *Nan-Shan*'s decks looked towards the bridge. Then he sighed, and with sudden resignation: "It would certainly be a dam' distressful sight", he said meekly.[8]

Jukes embodies the young Britisher's ardent patriotism and reverence for the Union Jack. MacWhirr, even though "so jolly innocent that if you were to put your thumb to your nose and wave your fingers at him he would only wonder gravely to himself what got into you",[9] represents a far more profound sense of security in being British. During the typhoon when Jukes voices his opinion as to the outcome of taking the spilled and rolling money away from the Chinamen in their storm-wrecked hold to stop their mad scrambling for its repossession, he says, "Let them only recover a bit, and you'll see. They will fly at our throats, sir. Don't forget, sir, she isn't a British ship now. These brutes know

8   *Ibid.*, pp. 9-11.
9   *Ibid.*, p. 18.

it well, too. The damned Siamese flag." MacWhirr answers him with British ponderosity which would be unmitigatedly offensive arrogance if it were not just completely unimaginative confidence in their being British: "We are on board, all the same".[10]

The Union Jack is used as a means of security by Almayer, a Dutchman in a Dutch territory, when the natives begin to stir up trouble. He later tells Lingard, "I had the Jack up since the morning and began to feel safer." [11] Jim-Eng, a Chinaman, carries the sense of security even further, to positive identification. He flatly refuses to bow to the Dutch flag raised by the Malays and Arabs and runs for his life into Almayer's compound under the "Jack". "Said he was an Englishman, and would not take off his hat to any flag but English." He would not even try to escape for his life. "He wouldn't. Not he. He was English, and he would fight the whole lot. Says he: 'They are only black fellows. We white men . . . can fight everybody in Sambir.' " [12] This is not as isolated a case as one might think. So potent is the power of the British to capture the imagination of Eastern peoples at times, that one of the main and most recurring problems of a well-known European portrait artist in Ceylon, a former British crown colony, as she told us in 1949, was to reproduce truthfully the color of native cabinet ministers and high government officials in their commissioned paintings. They were always shocked and rather hurt-surprised to see themselves represented as "so dark"! Their reaction was all the more surprising since their color was light, light enough for them often to be taken for Italians when they were in Europe. They must have envisaged themselves as having something close to the ruddy English coloring. That Orientals are color-conscious is not surprising when one remembers, as was pointed out to me by a Tamil gentleman, that the lower down the caste scale one goes, the darker the complexion becomes.

The pro-British bias is detected in Conrad's presentations of the various attitudes by whites toward Orientals. MacWhirr may adopt the British aloof consideration toward low-class Easterners,

[10] *Ibid.*, pp. 82-83.
[11] *An Outcast of the Islands*, p. 181.
[12] *Ibid.*, p. 182.

as when Jukes refers to the Chinese laborers in the hold as passengers: "The Chinamen! Why don't you speak plainly? Couldn't tell what you meant. Never heard a lot of coolies spoken of as passengers before. Passengers, indeed!" [13] But he also displays the British sense of responsibility for dependents and justice. As soon as he learns that the Chinamen and their boxes have broken loose and are together one big jumble because of the storm's violence, he sends Jukes down to do what he can for them. Jukes reports that he has rigged life lines and secured the money, adding pessimistically, since he firmly believes the ship will be torn apart by the typhoon, that "it may not matter in the end". Through the lashing wind, MacWhirr rebukes him: "Had to do what's fair, for all – they are only Chinamen. Give them the same chance with ourselves – hang it all." [14]

When the typhoon has passed, an equitable solution for the division of the Chinamen's money has to be arranged. The ship is in tatters and great amounts of work must be done. No one has been able to sleep for days. Jukes says to Captain MacWhirr, "I wish you would let us throw the whole lot of these dollars down to them and leave them to fight it out amongst themselves, while we get a rest." MacWhirr's heavy sense of duty prompts him to reply, "Now you talk wild, Jukes. . . . We must plan out something that would be fair to all parties." [15] In his sure and steady stolidity, he then does just that.

Jukes' attitude, in all his youth and excitability, "was gruff, as became his racial superiority, but not unfriendly".[16] In contrast to Jukes, the not very admirable crew of the *Nan-Shan* represents the gross approach of the insensible element of the European peoples, those who are not "one of us". Their concern was all for their own petty desire for a light when Jukes was involved with doing what he could for that "inextricable confusion of heads and shoulders, naked soles kicking upwards, fists raised, tumbling backs, legs, pigtails, faces". "On his passage back the hands in the alleyway swore at him for a fool. Why didn't he bring that

13   *Typhoon*, p. 31.
14   *Ibid.*, pp. 87-88.
15   *Ibid.*, p. 99.
16   *Ibid.*, p. 13.

lamp? What the devil did the coolies matter to anybody?" [17] This attitude, rejected by Conrad, is not limited to only the lower classes of British; yet when found in the upper class groups it exists among those who do not really know the East or who are incapable of any real sympathy for that part of the world or understanding of what this sympathy involves. Wealthy but doltish Mr. Travers is a good picture of the stupidity of official-dom removed from direct contact with its responsibility. At a time when everyone's life is in danger from native intrigue, and all possible intelligence is needed to avoid serious trouble, he can only spout:

"This coast", he began again, "has been placed under the sole protec-tion of Holland by the treaty of 1820. The treaty of 1820 creates special rites and obligations. . . . An international understanding – the duty to civilize – failed to carry out – compact –. . . ." Mr. Travers' voice went on dogmatic and obstinate for a long time. The end came with a certain vehemence.
"And if the inferior race must perish, it is a gain, a step towards the perfecting of society which is the aim of progress." [18]

The same derogatory judgment is passed on Shaw, unfamiliar with the East and mentally incapable of becoming otherwise. His views arise in a discussion with young Captain Lingard about war:

Sinful, the old gentleman [his grandfather] called it – and I think so, too. Unless with Chinamen, or niggers, or such people as must be kept in order and won't listen to reason; having not sense enough to know what's good for them, when it's explained to them by their betters – missionaries, and such like au-tho-ri-ties.[19]

Such empty ignorance and lack of any ability to discriminate is brought out in Shaw's reaction to finding Rajah Hassim and Princess Immada waiting in Lingard's cabin:

Suddenly his eyes became stony with amazement and indignation; he pointed a fat and trembling forefinger.
"Niggers", he said huskily. "In the cuddy! In the cuddy!" He appeared bereft of speech for a time. Since he entered the cabin Hassim had been watching him in thoughtful and expectant silence. "I can't have it", he continued with genuine feeling in his voice.

[17]   *Ibid.*, p. 58.
[18]   *The Rescue*, pp. 147-148.
[19]   *Ibid.*, p. 22.

"Damme! I've too much respect for myself." He rose with heavy deliberation; his eyes bulged out in a severe and dignified stare. "Out you go!" he bellowed, suddenly, making a step forward.[20]

Needless to say, he is made ridiculous. As an individual, he is far inferior to both Hassim and Immada – and to many of their state servants – since he lacks the attributes which make up the "distinction of being white".

A similar basic lack of intelligence is presented in the aunt, a wax flower product of pure conventionality, of the heroine in "The Planter of Malata". At one time in the story she prattles a lot of twaddle about London seances and apparitions. When Renouard, having actual trouble getting his coolies to labor in a part of the estate where a dead man is buried, remarks, " 'Those plantation boys of mine see ghosts too.' . . . The sister of the philosopher sat up stiffly. What crudeness! . . . 'Mr. Renouard! How can you compare the superstitious fancies of your horrible savages with the manifestations . . .!' " [21]

The enigmatic Captain Brierly in *Lord Jim*, who both apparently understands the most complex and sophisticated question of courage and its place in British society in the East, and fails as a compassionate human being, indicates his failure by the comment, "Frankly, I don't care a snap for all the pilgrims that ever came out of Asia, but a decent man would not have behaved like this to a full cargo of old rags in bales." [22] His concept of the "idea" is too removed from actual involvement. Unlike Captain MacWhirr, Brierly never performs an act which proves his words derogatory to Orientals are in reality a matter of being merely "gruff". And, unlike MacWhirr, Brierly is not "one of us". This statement may seem questionable when we consider all of the positive qualities he has that belong to "us"; but it becomes justifiable when we realize he lacks the "unselfish belief in the idea", since he commits the selfish act of suicide.

As I have indicated, most of the non-British characters in Conrad's works are either villains or failures. The non-British

---

[20]   *Ibid.*, p. 239.
[21]   *Ibid.*, p. 67.
[22]   *Lord Jim*, p. 68.

attitudes toward the East and Eastern peoples are also villainous
or failuristic. If any one thing were needed to make a man
reluctant to accept the "burden", it would be knowledge of the
early Belgian control in Africa, the depths of depravity to which
unethical power can descend. The greedy Company in *Heart of
Darkness* speaks of the independent ivory trader: " 'We will not
be free from unfair competition till one of these fellows is hanged
for an example', he said. 'Certainly', grunted the other; 'get him
hanged! Why not? Anything – anything can be done in this
country.' " [23] One of the independent traders who had nursed
Kurtz in his physical illness speaks to Marlow about the former
patient:

He declared he would shoot me unless I gave him the ivory and then
cleared out of the country, because he could do so, and had a fancy
for it, and there was nothing on earth to prevent him killing whom he
jolly well pleased. And it was true, too. I gave him the ivory.[24]

This attitude toward their own race being dominant, it takes little
imagination to call up a picture of such an organization's approach to the "blacks". The same trader has this to say when he
learns of the Company's possible plot to hang him: "What's to
stop them?" [25] The only force which could stop them from all
their excess of unrestraint – robbery, slaughter of natives, both by
overwork and brutal, senseless violence – would be recognition of
and a respect for the "idea". Correlated to the Belgian attitude is
Conrad's comment on the French control in adjacent areas:

Once I remember, we came upon a man-of-war anchored off the
coast. There wasn't even a shed there, and she was shelling the bush.
It appears the French had one of their wars going on thereabouts. Her
ensign dropped limp like a rag; the muzzles of the long six-inch guns
stuck out all over the low hull; the greasy, slimy swell swung her up
lazily and let her down, swaying her thin masts. In the empty immen-
sity of earth, sky, and water, there she was, incomprehensible, firing
into a continent. Pop, would go one of the six-inch guns; a small flame
would dart and vanish, a little white smoke would disappear, a tiny
projectile would give a feeble screech – and nothing happened. Nothing could happen. There was a touch of insanity in the proceeding, a

[23]   *Heart of Darkness*, p. 91.
[24]   *Ibid.*, p. 128.
[25]   *Ibid.*, p. 139.

sense of lugubrious drollery in the sight; and it was not dissipated by somebody on board assuring me earnestly there was a camp of natives – he called them enemies! – hidden out of sight somewhere.[26]

In *Victory*, Conrad describes Schomberg and Ricardo: "Both these white men looked on native life as a mere play of shadows the dominant race could walk through unaffected and disregarded in the pursuit of its incomprehensible aims and needs." [27] The German captain of the *Patna* "brutalized all those he was not afraid of, and wore a 'blood-and-iron' air, combined with a purple nose and a red moustache".[28] We have already been exposed to the depraved attitude of Kurtz and the Belgian administration in Africa. As for Dutch Willems:

He fancied that nothing would be changed, that he would be able as heretofore to tyrannize good-humouredly over his half-caste wife, to notice with tender contempt his pale yellow child, to patronize loftily his dark-skinned brother-in-law, who loved pink neckties and wore patent-leather boots on his little feet, and was so humble before the white husband of the lucky sister. Those were the delights of his life, and he was unable to conceive that the moral significance of any act of his could interfere with the very nature of things, could dim the light of the sun, could destroy the perfume of the flowers, the submission of his wife, the smile of his child, the awe-struck respect of Leonard da Souza and of all the Da Souza family. That family's admiration was the great luxury of his life. It rounded and completed his existence in a perpetual assurance of unquestionable superiority. He loved to breathe the coarse incense they offered before the shrine of the successful white man. ... It gives one a feeling of enormously remote superiority, and Willems revelled in it. .... Probably his greatest delight lay in the unexpressed but intimate conviction that, should he close his hand, all those admiring human beings would starve.[29]

He is so unreceptive to intelligences other than his own that he is quite incapable of seeing his reversed position with regard to his wife's "tribe" when he is fallen from his pedestal, aided by a few shoves from Leonard, who helped expose Willems' thefts. " 'Why, Captain Lingard', he burst out, 'the fellow licked my boots'." It remains for Lingard to explain to him why Leonard aided his

26   *Ibid.*, pp. 61-62.
27   *Victory*, p. 167.
28   *Lord Jim*, p. 14.
29   *An Outcast of the Islands*, pp. 3-5.

downfall: " 'Yes, yes, yes', said Lingard, testily, 'we know that, and you did your best to cram your boot down his throat. No man likes that, my boy.' " [30]

A Yankee-American salesman's attitude toward handling the race problem is introduced by his comment on "a man with hooked features and of German extraction who was supposed to be agent for a Dutch crockery house", but was suspected by the other traders to be a Dutch spy:

"Is that so?" asked a New England voice. "Why don't you let daylight into him?"

"Oh we can't do that here", murmured one of the players. "Your deal Trench, let us get on."

"Can't you?" drawled the New England voice, "you law-abiding, get-a-summons, act-of-parliament lot of sons of Belial – can't you? Now, look a-here, these Colt pistols I am selling –" He took the pearler aside and could be heard talking earnestly in the corner. "See-you load-and-see?" There were rapid clicks. "Simple, isn't it? And if any trouble – say with your divers –" *click, click, click* – "Through and through – like a sieve – warranted to cure the worst kind of cussedness in any nigger." [31]

Conrad's indirect criticism of the non-British attitude, the lack of "idea", is well summed up in the criticism of the British approach to the South American race problem by Decoud, a "Frenchified" South American: "Life is not for me a moral romance derived from the tradition of a pretty fairy tale." [32]

That the white man "keep face", maintain his superior position, is not only insisted upon by the whites, particularly the British, but is fully expected by the natives. "Keeping face" involves the deep issues of identity, pride, trust, courage, assumption of responsibility; therefore, its concern with the superficial and external aspects gathers great importance because of what the incidentals represent.

The British concept of dress in the colonial areas of the world has been, and still is to a lesser degree, a source of humor. They seem to have made attire a concern of greater importance than have other colonizers. As recently as the late 1940's and early

[30]   *Ibid.*, p. 33.
[31]   *The Rescue*, p. 96.
[32]   *Nostromo: A Tale of the Seaboard*, p. 218.

1950's, executives of American oil firms in Ceylon and India were advised to wear white drill suits as office attire. So fixed in the minds of the colonial and national members of the society was the matter of dress, that white shoes were admonished against as being a mark of the Anglo-Indian – that is, in its present usage, the half-caste. Therefore, the matter of keeping up appearances is not a superficial matter of stuffiness as much as it is a concern for identity. Neat white clothing is, as a result, a mark of the Sahib in the East, and becomes second nature to those who occupy such a position in the Orient or any other colonial area. There is good reason for such clothing. It is cool and it can more easily than some other color of material be determined clean or not. Conrad, both consciously and unconsciously as part of his *milieu*, utilizes again and again throughout his fiction the symbol of not only white clothes, but the state of clothes in general.

In all of the morass of corruption upon approaching the heart of darkness, Marlow finds but one man who represents something for which he can have genuine respect. He makes his way through the tangle of inefficiency and the overworked, dying blacks that clutter the path to the company's compound:

When near the buildings I met a white man, in such an unexpected elegance of get-up that in the first moment I took him for a sort of vision. I saw a high starched collar, white cuffs, a light alpaca jacket, snowy trousers, a clean necktie, and varnished boots. No hat. Hair parted, brushed, oiled, under a green-lined parasol held in a big white hand. He was amazing. . . . I wouldn't have mentioned the fellow to you at all, only it was from his lips that I first heard the name of the man who is so indissolubly connected with the memories of that time. Moreover, I respected the fellow. Yes; I respected his collars, his vast cuffs, his brushed hair. His appearance was certainly that of a hair-dresser's dummy; but in the great demoralization of the land he kept up his appearance. That's backbone. His starched collars and got-up shirt-fronts were achievements of character. He had been out nearly three years; and, later I could not help asking him how he managed to sport such linen. He had just the faintest blush, and said modestly, "I've been teaching one of the native women about the station. It was difficult. She had a distaste for the work." Thus this man had verily accomplished something.[33]

[33] *Heart of Darkness*, pp. 67-68.

This chief-accountant is unique in his surroundings. He is the only one who represents the British attitude of proper personal appearance, one of the greatest aides to self respect. Such appearance as the above, as Marlow points out, does take effort in primitive surroundings, and indicates no in-road of decay on one's identity.

In the same African setting, the disintegration of white Kazerts and Carlier is given us in the description of their bedroom. "The plank floor was littered with the belongings of the white men; . . . torn wearing apparel, old boots; all the things dirty, and all the things broken, that accumulate mysteriously round untidy men." [34]

Clothing in the East is not so much the morality of covering the body as it is a convention of wealth, caste, social position, official prestige, and other considerations of the complex conventions of anciently evolved societies. Ultimately it all comes to one's identity, which includes the consideration of others' identities. Karain was most attractive when he came on his informal calls. "He was simplicity itself then; all in white; muffled about his head; for arms only a kriss with a plain buffalo-horn handle, which he would politely conceal within a fold of his sarong before stepping over the threshold." [35] We can now better understand the turmoil going on within Arsat before we are told anything about it. His first appearance is given starkly, but we can read the situation by the condition of his costume. "He had nothing on but his sarong. His head was bare." [36] Now in the East there is nothing to seeing a man in a sarong only, but Arsat is from a proud and well-known family, therefore a jacket or open vest of some sort would be expected, to give him social identity.[37] He is

---

[34] "An Outpost of Progress", in *Tales of Unrest*, p. 87

[35] "Karain: A Memory", p. 11.

[36] "The Lagoon", in *Tales of Unrest*, p. 190.

[37] In 1950 an incident took place in Ceylon involving a member of a caste not permitted to wear a jacket. In a fit of extravagant desire for adornment, the person appeared in public in a jacket. The national (a term preferred to "native") townspeople immediately administered a sound thrashing to the unwise one right on the street to impress on him the impropriety of appearing in public in a jacket instead of decorously bare-chested. The indecorum was not repeated. The rule of custom applied to both male and female members of the caste. In the areas where this

Moslem; therefore a Fez or small cloth turban is expected, to give him religious identity. The reader who knows these facts of Eastern custom knows that something is very wrong with Arsat's condition, which turns out to be the case as the story later develops. A very subtle device of forewarning.

The vapidity of the delicate lady aunt in "The Planter of Malata" is brought out in her dislike for the functional and working costume of the responsible Sahib or Master. "She did not like him very much in the afternoons, in his white drill suit and planter's hat. . . ." [38] But in the evening when he was in a dinner jacket, it was another matter.

The narrator of "Because of the Dollars" notices Davidson because he is not in the usual costume. "He attracted my attention because in the movement of figures in white drill suits on the pavement from which he stepped, his costume, the usual tunic and trousers, being made of light grey flannel, made him noticeable." [39] And he is apart and different, for "Davidson alone was visibly married". [40]

In *Victory*, to indicate what a distraught state Morrison is in over the possibility of losing his ship to some Portugese colonial officials, the author describes the man's attire: "His white clothes, which he had not taken off for three days, were dingy. He looked already gone to the bad, past redemption. The sight was shocking. . . ." [41] Such a sight would be shocking indeed, for Morrison was the type of man who normally would change his "whites" at least once and quite often twice a day.

Heyst's basic decency is demonstrated by the fact that, "He looked exactly as we have always seen him – very neat, white shoes, cork helmet." [42] His white costume later takes on a sym-

---

particular caste were numerous, both British and American military vehicle accident rates were high during World War II because of eyes' being engaged not on the roads, but on national anatomies. The situation became so serious that the caste ban was relaxed and jackets were allowed the lowly. However, custom prevailed, decorum was followed, bosoms were bared, and trucks continued to run off the roads.

[38]   "The Planter of Malata", p. 44.
[39]   "Because of the Dollars", p. 169.
[40]   *Ibid.*, p. 175.
[41]   *Victory*, p. 13.   [42]   *Ibid.*, p. 28.

bolic angelic quality, making him appear as a divine member of the heavenly host sent by God at just the right time to save Morrison. He, "staring open-mouthed, groped over his shoulder for the cord of the eyeglass hanging down his back. When he found it, he stuck it in his eye hastily. It was as if he expected Heyst's usual white suit of the tropics to change into a shining garment flowing down to his toes. . . ." [43]

In the same novel, the rather dense Schomberg is taken in by the outward symbol of identity as he observes plain Mr. Jones and Ricardo. "Both he and his long, lank principal wore the usual white suit of the tropics, cork helmets, pipe-clayed white shoes — all correct." [44]

Marlow first notices Jim in the group of *Patna* officers because, "there he stood, clean-limbed, clean-faced. . . ." [45] The beginning of the book itself tells us in the fourth sentence, "He was spotlessly neat, apparelled in immaculate white from shoes to hat. . . ." [46] Jim maintains to the end his British appearance, even in that most remote area of his exiled life. Such propriety is to his intrinsic credit, even though it assisted in his physical downfall, by antagonizing a cheap villain; for "there was something in the very neatness of Jim's clothes, from the white helmet to the canvass leggings and the pipe-clayed shoes, which in Brown's sombre irritated eyes seemed to belong to things he had in the very shaping of his life contemned and flouted".[47] The final view Marlow has of Jim in which he is symbolically "white from head to foot" [48] is dealt with elsewhere in this study.

In the case of Jorgenson's return to life by going back into the world of white men to assume active administration, he no longer appears "dressed in faded blue serge and without any kind of linen",[49] but appears as an embodiment of the essence of one who takes up the white man's burden:

[43] *Ibid.*, p. 16.
[44] *Ibid.*, p. 100.
[45] *Lord Jim*, p. 40.
[46] *Ibid.*, p. 3.
[47] *Ibid.*, p. 380.
[48] *Ibid.*, p. 336.
[49] *The Rescue*, p. 91.

In the early morning light, white from head to foot in a perfectly clean suit of clothes which seemed hardly to contain any limbs, freshly shaven (Jörgenson's sunken cheeks with their withered colouring always had a sort of gloss as though he had the habit of shaving every two hours or so) he looked as immaculate as though he had been indeed a pure spirit superior to the soiling contacts of the material earth.[50]

To this man who had gone completely native before his return to life, there was still the concern for identity in the appearance of white people, even the wealthy, attractive wife of the owner of the stranded yacht.

To Jörgenson Mrs. Travers in her un-European dress had always been displeasing, almost monstrous. Her stature, her gestures, her general carriage [Western women's notoriously bad posture is displayed even more prominently in Eastern clothes] struck his eye as absurdly incongruous with a Malay costume, too ample, too free, too bold – offensive.[51]

The criticism works both ways. With regard to the native crew of the brig, "only one or two wore sarongs, the others having submitted – at least at sea – to the indignity of European trousers." [52]

The clothing supplied Mrs. Travers to take the place of her own symbolizes the conflict of attention within the young Lingard, for the rich Malay attire was heretofore being saved for Princess Immada upon her return to her rightful rule. Mrs. Travers is not unaware of the turmoil. " 'I am robbing the girl of her clothes', she had thought to herself, 'besides other things'. She knew by this time that a girl of such high rank would never dream of wearing anything that had been worn by somebody else." [53] An Oriental social convention is used here to enhance the presentation of friction between the two women of different blood, whereas the breaking of the same convention intensifies the presentation of genuine rapport between two men of different blood when Hollis gives his dry sarong to Karain.

The initial personal appearance of Shaw, the unlikeable chief mate to young Captain Lingard of *Rescue*, indicates a weakness

50 *Ibid.*, p. 248.
51 *Ibid.*, p. 363.
52 *Ibid.*, p. 13.
53 *Ibid.*, p. 385.

of character: "On his bare feet he wore a pair of straw sandals, and his head was protected by an enormous pith hat – once white but now very dirty. . . ." [54] That he, as an individual, is interested in only the outward aspect of his superior position as a European is shown in part when he appears "clad in a spotless white suit" [55] to meet the disabled yacht.

We know that Almayer has "gone native", not only from the way his household is managed, but also when before his guests, European naval officers, he appears dressed "in his white jacket and flowered sarong".[56] Willems' reversion to a primitive life, his absolute collapse, is given a repulsive note as he creeps back from his jungle love-nest, "a masquerading spectre of the once so very confidential clerk of the richest merchant in the islands. His jacket was soiled and torn; below the waist he was clothed in a worn-out and faded sarong." [57] The non-fictional Willems was, though an outcast, Conrad tells us, "clad always in a spotless sleeping suit".[58] In *Nostromo*, although not of an Eastern setting but treating the subject of Conrad's colonialism, the bitter Dr. Monygham eccentrically appeared in articles of attire which

were an established defiance to the conventionalities of Sulaco. Had it not been for the immaculate clean linen of his apparel he might have been taken for one of those shiftless Europeans that are a moral eyesore to the respectability of a foreign colony in almost every exotic part of the world. The young ladies of Sulace . . . would remark to each other, "Here is the Señor doctor going to call on Doña Amilia. He has got his little coat on." . . . The little white jacket was in reality a concession to Mrs. Gould's humanizing influence.[59]

The matter of dress in Conrad is one indication of a civilized, "humanizing" ceremoniousness and an intrinsic discipline quite rightly expected of any group which assumes the responsibility of correctly administering others. It is indicative of a discipline of identity.

As another aid in keeping "face", the white man must keep

[54]   *Ibid.*, p. 6.
[55]   *Ibid.*, p. 53.
[56]   *Almayer's Folly*, p. 35.
[57]   *An Outcast of the Islands*, p. 87.
[58]   *Ibid.*, p. ix.
[59]   *Nostromo: A Tale of the Seaboard*, p. 45.

himself somewhat aloof; to do that, he must keep himself separate. On the old ship deliberately beached in order that it could be
used as a warehouse for explosives and other supplies, "Jörgenson,
on taking up his dead command, had a house of thin boards built
on the after deck for his own accommodation and that of Lingard
during his flying visits to the Shore of Refuge." Since we know
Jörgenson, "if he did sleep at all, – slept very little", and that
Lingard always slept on deck, "the erection of that primitive
deckhouse was a matter of propriety rather than of necessity. It
was proper that the white men should have a place to themselves
on board." [60] As proper, "one end of the Casa Viola ... was
reserved for the English engineers" while the other was kept for
"the select clientele of engine-drivers and foremen of the railway
shops", of Italian blood.[61] It is well to remember that engineers
in England do not have, in general, the same professional or
social rank as engineers in the U.S.A. In *Nostromo* the English
were paid this respect – the "reserved end" – even though the
Casa Viola was "the Italian stronghold".

"Loss of face" is the reason Brierly is extremely agitated about
the legal trial of Jim. He argues with Marlow in an attempt to
secure contributions to ship Jim immediately out of the country
away from the courts.

"This infernal publicity is too shocking: there he sits while all these
confounded natives, serangs, lascars, quartermasters, are giving evidence that's enough to burn a man to ashes with shame. This is
abominable. ... If he went away all this would stop at once." ...
"The worst of it", he said, "is that all you fellows have no sense of
dignity; you don't think enough of what you are supposed to be". ...
"We are trusted." [62]

If Conrad's philosophy in specific application to his presentation
of colonial society is ignored in reading the above passage, Brierly
appears in a very bad light indeed. His own code would appear
to be one of insufferable stuffiness and out and out hypocrisy, in
that he seems to say the truth lies only in appearances. We know

[60]   *The Rescue*, pp. 263-264.
[61]   *Nostromo: A Tale of the Seaboard*, p. 32.
[62]   *Lord Jim*, pp. 67-68.

that he does not believe this since he, appearing to be the epitome
of self-assured strong success, commits suicide when he realizes he
does not have the strength in him to stand the test presented in
Heart of Darkness. But Brierly, manipulated by Conrad and
presented as deficient in some qualities necessary to facing up to
the "burden", is shown here to have a profound insight into
colonial society which Jim lacks. Brierly is able to weigh the
value of Jim's innocent egocentric devotion to standing up and
taking his medicine like a man, and the degree of destruction
Jim's idealistic devotion to himself causes to the reputation of the
society to which he belongs. And our answer lies here. The white
colonial society standing for what it does, counts in Brierly's
judgment as more important than the individual. Conrad has already made clear in *Heart of Darkness* that the individual is
important only in relation with what he belongs to, instead of
vice-versa. Jim, being "one of us", is therefore less important than
"us". His act is in effect a lump of rotting hippo meat which must
be buried and put out of sight; for what good is accomplished for
the order of things to leave it lying exposed? Brierly is merely
carrying out Conrad's belief that it is our duty and purpose to go
about burying the rotten flesh. If Jim were not there, he still
would be tried and punished, but the spectacle would be missing.
Therefore, in Conrad's eyes, Brierly's stand is more moral and
ethical than it is less. He is serving in a very perceptive manner
the "idea", which Conrad at no time claims is a perfect concept,
but one which can "save us".

Naturally, Conrad's theme discussed above has greater universal application than to colonial society alone, but it is presented
in that context.

Lingard does have a sense of "dignity" and "what he is supposed to be"; so much so that he can almost sympathize with
Willems with regard to the incentives for the latter's attempted
suicide. Willems has been thrown out of his job because he has
been caught in thievery, as well as been made a fool of by Hudig
with regard to Hudig's illegitimate daughter, Willems' wife. Because he is partially responsible for Willems' being in the area of
Malaya he is, there may be a double meaning as Lingard says, "I

am almost ashamed of myself, but I can understand your dirty pride." [63]

This sense of a tight bond of inter-responsibility and dependence among white people to help each other maintain "face", which does not exist as so strong a bond among the Orientals, is repeated in Jukes' plan to control all the Chinese coolies. He wanted to keep them under battened hatches until they reached Fu-chow. "We would find there, most likely, some sort of man-of-war, and once under her guns we were safe enough; for surely any skipper of a man-of-war – English, French, or Dutch – would see white men through as far as row on board goes." [64]

The fullest description in Conrad of an Englishman keeping his English identity, which he must do if he wishes to have any "face", in non-English surroundings lies in the portrayal of Charles Gould.

. . . The Gould family, established in Costaguana for three generations, always went to England for their education and for their wives. . . .

Born in the country, as his father before him, spare and tall, with a flaming moustache, a neat chin, clear blue eyes, auburn hair, and a thin, fresh, red face, Charles Gould looked like a new arrival from over the sea. His grandfather had fought in the cause of independence under Bolivar, in that famous English legion which on the battlefield of Carabobo had been saluted by the great Liberator as saviours of his country. One of Charles Gould's uncles had been the elected President of that province of Sulaco (then called a State) in the days of the Federation, and afterwards had been put up against the wall of a church and shot by the order of the barbarous Unionist general, Guzman Bento. . . . With such a family record, no one could be more of a Costaguanero than Don Carlos Gould; but his aspect was so characteristic that in the talk of common people he was just the Inglez – the Englishman of Sulaco. He looked more English than a casual tourist, a sort of heretic pilgrim, however, quite unknown in Sulaco. He looked more English than the last arrived batch of young railway engineers, than anybody out of the hunting-field pictures in the numbers of *Punch* reaching his wife's drawingroom two months or so after date. . . . There was something so indelible in all these ancestral Goulds – liberators, explorers, coffee planters, merchants, revolutionists – of Costaguana, that he, the only representative of the third generation in a continent possessing its own style of horsemanship, went on looking

[63] *An Outcast of the Islands*, p. 40.
[64] *Typhoon*, p. 98.

thoroughly English even on horseback. . . . Charles Gould, to use the suitably lofty phrase, rode like a centaur. Riding for him was not a special form of exercise; it was a natural faculty, as walking straight is to all men sound of mind and limb; but, all the same, when cantering beside the rutty ox-cart track to the mine he looked in his English clothes and with his imported saddlery as though he had come this moment to Costaguana at his easy swift *pasatrote*, straight out of some green meadow at the other side of the world. . . .

Don Carlos Gould, in his English clothes, looked as incongruous, but much more at home than the kindly cavalier [Charles IV] reining in his steed on the pedestal above the sleeping leperos, with his marble arm raised towards the marble rim of a plumed hat.

The weather-stained effigy of the mounted king, with its vague suggestion of a saluting gesture, seemed to present an inscrutable breast to the political changes which had robbed it of its very name; but neither did the other horseman, well known to the people, keen and alive on his well-shaped, slate-coloured beast with a white eye, wear his heart on the sleeve of his English coat. His mind preserved its steady poise as if sheltered in the passionless stability of private and public decencies at home in Europe. He accepted with a like calm the shocking manner in which the Sulaco ladies smothered their faces with pearl powder till they looked like white plaster casts with beautiful living eyes, the peculiar gossip of the town, and the continuous political changes, the constant "saving of the country", which to his wife seemed a puerile and bloodthirsty game of murder and rapine played with terrible earnestness by depraved children.[65]

The fact that "face" is all-important in the East, particularly to the white man since his real position is based on it, enables Conrad to use it as a goading and gnawing antagonism in two of his most powerful "retribution" scenes. The white man could have been and could be at any time outnumbered in the Orient and reduced to nothing. Since honesty as we know it is one of the requirements for him to maintain "face", and not required of Orientals, he can never build up the huge personal fortunes as can the native residents of the East. This, added to the fact that

---

[65] *Nostromo: A Tale of the Seaboard*, pp. 46-49. Conrad's insistence may appear somewhat exaggerated; however, British conduct in South America today supports the description. A delightful old friend of mine, Argentinean by nationality, British by blood, told me at a Christmas party in Ceylon in 1948, that the long established British colony in Argentina makes a habit of speaking Spanish with atrocious accents to maintain their identity, even though they can speak the language perfectly correctly.

he is expected to pay more for articles and servants, prevents him
from depending on wealth for his distinction. He therefore must
fall back on his being what he is for his position. Almayer
realizes his chance to bring Willems to the lowest of the low as
payment for all the worry and torment his presence has caused
him when the latter – barefoot, filthy, unshaven, and underfed –
comes crawling out of the jungle to beg a favor. Almayer taunts
Willems: " 'Now you are here you are not pretty to look at.' 'Let
me speak, will you!' exclaimed Willems.

"   'Don't shout like this. Do you think yourself in the forest
with your. . . . friends? This is a civilized man's house. A white
man's. Understand?' " [66] After hurling the word "understand",
usually the final word in any rebuke to an Eastern servant and a
word not used at all when talking with equals, Almayer raves
on: " 'You are as estimable as a heap of garbage. . . . Even
father, even Captain Lingard [notorious for his assisting sunken
and debased human beings] would not touch you now with a
pair of tongs; not with a ten-foot pole.' " [67] The last shred of any
respect he might be due is removed from Willems when Almayer
shoves him off the porch like any dog, kicks his hat after him,
and has Nina, a female child, call out after the running figure,
before all the servants and men in the compound, in a region of
the Moslem faith: "Pig! Pig! Pig!" [68]

But Willems gets his revenge in a sequel to the native attack
on Almayer's compound. Almayer, in a rage, tells Lingard:

By his orders they laid me out on the floor, wrapped me in my
hammock, and he started to stitch me in, as if I had been a corpse,
beginning at the feet. While he worked he laughed wickedly. I called
him all the names I could think of. He told them to put their dirty
paws over my mouth and nose. I was nearly choked. Whenever I
moved they punched me in the ribs. He went on taking fresh needle-
fuls as he wanted them, and working steadily. Sewed me up to my
throat. Then he rose, saying, "That will do; let go." That woman had
been standing by; they must have been reconciled. She clapped her
hands. I lay on the floor like a bale of goods while he stared at me,
and the woman shrieked with delight. Like a bale of goods! There was

[66]   *An Outcast of the Islands*, p. 88.
[67]   *Ibid.*, p. 91.
[68]   *Ibid.*, p. 94.

a grin on every face, and the verandah was full of them. I wished myself dead – 'pon my word, Captain Lingard, I did! I do now whenever I think of it.[69]

For his own pride it would have been better if he had died, for the native woman "capered before [him] and made faces; snapped her fingers before [his] nose". This lack of respect, and from a woman, was so great as to shame the native men who had just been insulting him.[70]

---

[69]   *Ibid.*, pp. 183-184.
[70]   *Idem.*

VI

CONRAD'S SYMPATHETIC IDENTIFICATION OF MERCHANT-ADVENTURERS WITH THE CONSTRUCTIVE APPLICATION OF ANGLO-SAXON ADMINISTRATIVE SUPERIORITY

It is not surprising that Conrad's presentation of the white man's burden is closely related to the commercial life of the East and in such relation receives his most sympathetic treatment. He is not always as tolerant of white supremacy as found in the very top planes of officialdom. Often, there, one encounters great pomp and show with very little else to accompany it since direct contact with end results is almost impossible at that level of statecraft. There is a suggestion, too, in his works, that the sea captains and merchants can practice the doctrines of Conrad's colonialism without necessarily treading too heavily on formal political liberties or establishments. His greatest heroes all have expansive political power, but only because of their own individual worth and efforts to work with what does exist and to influence such existing political factions. They do not have the strength of the British State Government to back them up, but the strength of Anglo-Saxon qualities. Another consideration is the fact that top colonial governmental officials do not act and react according to their own dictates of conscience and judgment, but do as their State Governments direct them. It is difficult to imagine Conrad interested in or sympathetic with men who, in the situations with which he deals, are mere mouthpieces for a home office and not individuals at all. His contacts, too, were limited to merchant adventurers and men who were in commerce what they made of themselves and were not corporation executives who ascend the ladder not so much through their own abilities as through the emptying of the next rung above – a process of advancement which time makes inevitable.

Since commerce to Conrad did involve dealing with other human beings, it was not just a matter of profit and loss. It enabled a man to be a complete individual. He could make his living, have adventure, and exert his pressure on the world around him. This concept is made clear in a verbal blast the merchant-adventurer hero Lingard directs at Travers, one of the most offensive portrayals of officialdom in Conrad. " 'I *am* an adventurer', he burst out, 'and if I hadn't been an adventurer, I would have had to starve or work at home for such people as you. If I weren't an adventurer, you would be most likely lying dead on this deck with your cut throat gaping at the sky.' " [1] The same idea is stated in a remark by Marlow about merchant-adventurer Stein, one of Conrad's noblest secondary characters. "There were very few places in the Archipelago he had not seen in the original dusk of their being, before light (and even electric light) had been carried into them for the sake of better morality and – and – well – the greater profit, too." [2]

Stein's business organization covered a vast area and had out-post stations in the remotest places, but Conrad well realizes that successful big business is not restricted to the whites in the East. Great business establishments existed in the East long before the West conceived of such commercial arrangements. As noble in his way as Stein, Abdullah held the reins of

a business that was spread over all the Archipelago: from Sumatra to New Guinea, from Batavia to Palawan. Very soon his ability, his will – strong to obstinacy – his wisdom beyond his years, caused him to be recognized as the head of a family whose members and connections were found in every part of those seas. An uncle here – a brother there; a father-in-law in Batavia, another in Palembang; husbands of numerous sisters; cousins innumerable scattered north, south, east, and west – in every place where there was trade: the great family lay like a network over the islands. They lent money to princes, influenced the council-rooms, faced – if need be – with peaceful intrepidity the white rulers who held the land and the sea under the edge of sharp swords; and they all paid great deference to Abdulla, listened to his

1   *The Rescue*, p. 134.
2   *Lord Jim*, p. 219.

advice, entered into his plans – because he was wise, pious, and fortunate.[3]

But the Arabs were not devoted to nor inspired by the "idea". It was not in them and they could not clearly see that it existed in others since their attitude was closely aligned with the piratical people of Arsat, who said, "We are of a people who take what they want – like you whites." [4] Since the "idea" was not part of their comprehension they could not be expected to realize its value; it seemed merely foolish and naïve. "Where they traded they would be masters and suffer no rival." [5] It therefore took more than the weak Almayer had in him to oppose them in commerce. "Almayer went on struggling desperately, but with a feebleness of purpose depriving him of all chance of success against men so unscrupulous and resolute as his rivals the Arabs." [6] The day before the great betrayal by Willems which would wipe out the business of Lingard and Almayer, Sahamin, a venerable patriarch of the Arab merchant community of Sambir, cogitated over his business plans:

Meantime it would be a good thing to interview Almayer to-morrow and, profiting by the last day of the hated man's prosperity, obtain some goods from him on credit. Sahamin thought it could be done by skillful wheedling. After all, that son of Satan was a fool, and the thing was worth doing, because the coming revolution would wipe all debts out. Sahamin did not mind imparting that idea to his companions, with much senile chuckling, while they strolled together from the riverside towards the residence.[7]

To the Arab, a perfectly ethical business maneuver. This same man reached a pitch of sincere indignation bordering on hysteria a few days earlier when the monstrous suggestion was made that he pay his debts:

That white man – may the grave of his mother be defiled! – is not content to hold us all in his hand with a cruel grasp. He seeks to cause our very death. He trades with the Dyaks of the forest, who are no better than monkeys. He buys from them guttah and rattan – while

---

[3]   *An Outcast of the Islands*, pp. 109-110.
[4]   "The Lagoon", in *Tales of Unrest*, p. 196.
[5]   *Almayer's Folly*, p. 24.
[6]   *Ibid.*, p. 25.
[7]   *An Outcast of the Islands*, pp. 136-137.

we starve. Only two days ago I went to him and said, "Tuan Almayer"
– even so; we must speak politely to that friend of Satan – "Tuan
Almayer, I have such and such goods to sell. Will you buy?" And he
spoke thus – because those white men have no understanding of any
courtesy – he spoke to me as if I was a slave: "Daoud, you are a lucky
man" – remark, O First among the Believers! that by those words he
could have brought misfortune on my head – "you are a lucky man to
have anything in these hard times. Bring your goods quickly, and I
shall receive them in payment of what you owe me from last year."
And he laughed, and struck me on the shoulder with his open hand.
May Jehannum be his lot! [8]

The destruction of his trade and collapse of his trading station
occur while Lingard is away on another expedition. When he
returns he immediately realizes the situation and dismisses his own
misfortune with little thought. His main concern is for the settlement of Sambir and their prospects under Arab control. "Great
pity. They will suffer for it. He will squeeze them. Great pity.
Damn it! I feel so sorry for them if I had the *Flash* here I would
try force. Eh!" [9] Lingard's position as merchant and counselor to
the people of Sambir is comparable to that of Stein and the
Scotsman whom Stein replaced in Patusan:

He came into the council-hall where all the rajahs, pangerans, and
headmen were assembled, with the queen, a fat wrinkled woman (very
free in her speech, Stein said) reclining on a high couch under a
canopy. He dragged his leg, thumping with his stick, and grasped
Stein's arm, leading him right up to the couch. "Look, queen, and you
rajahs, this is my son", he proclaimed in a stentorian voice. "I have
traded with your fathers, and when I die he shall trade with you and
your sons."

By means of this simple formality Stein inherited the Scotsman's
privileged position and all his stock-in-trade, together with a fortified
house on the banks of the only navigable river in the country. [10]

It need hardly be mentioned that such a position in the community could not be gained and held by a white man on only a business
basis of approach. Lingard voices his feelings of responsibility for
his commercial community to Willems as he sails out of the port
in which Willems was disgraced:

[8]   *Ibid.*, p. 116.
[9]   *Ibid.*, p. 173.
[10]   *Lord Jim*, p. 206.

"Here, Willems", he said calling him to his side, "d'ye see that barque here? That's an Arab vessel. White men have mostly given up the game, but this fellow drops in my wake often, and lives in hopes of cutting me out in that settlement. Not while I live, I trust. You see, Willems, I brought prosperity to that place. I composed their quarrels, and saw them grow under my eyes. There's peace and happiness there. I am more master there than his Dutch Excellency down in Batavia ever will be when some day a lazy man-of-war blunders at last against the river. I mean to keep the Arabs out of it, with their lies and their intrigues. I shall keep the venomous breed out, if it cost me my fortune.[11]

Such is the well-being which Willems betrays.

The Anglo-Saxon commercial influence on the politics and personal life in a non-European country is one of the main themes, if not the main theme, in the magnificent book *Nostromo*. Since I have stated that from the fifth chapter on, Conrad's various works will be treated under the headings of different phases of the "burden", it will be impossible to discuss completely each book as a unit. The next few sentences, therefore, in keeping with the commercial aspect of the thesis topic, will be about the Gould silver mine. The San Tomé mine was "the biggest thing in Sulaco, and even in the whole Republic. It was indeed a fabulous-ly rich mine. Its so-called agent, evidently a man of culture and ability, seemed, without official position, to possess an extra-ordinary influence in the highest Government spheres." [12] The mine property itself had been a tool of the Costaguana govern-ment, forced on Charles Gould's father as a machine of revenge and extortion, and the cause of his death. The South American Costaguana government – "the fourth in six years" – at the time of the "bestowal" of the mine on the elder Gould, showed an unusual insight into their intrinsic inability to practice business administration. "It remembered the San Tomé mine with a secret conviction of its worthlessness in their own hands. . . ." [13] Under the cool control of Charles Gould, the Inglez, the "King of Sulaco", "the San Tomé administration had, in part, at least, financed the last revolution, which had brought into a five-year

[11] *An Outcast of the Islands*, pp. 44-45.
[12] *Nostromo: A Tale of the Seaboard*, p. 38.
[13] *Ibid.*, p. 53.

dictatorship Don Vincente Ribiera, a man of culture and un-
blemished character, invested with a mandate of reform by the
best elements of the State. Serious, well-informed men seemed to
believe the fact, to hope for better things, for the establishment
of legality, of good faith and order in public life." [14] Because of
the existence of the mine and the fact that "the administrator of
the San Tomé silver mine had an immense influence over all these
Spanish Dons",[15] Sir John, Chairman of the Board of a railway,
and the Scots engineer-in-chief of the same outfit, were brought
together in the out-of-the-way province of Sulaco.

From the contact of these two personalities, who had not the same
vision of the world, there was generated a power for the world's
service – a subtle force that could set in motion mighty machines,
men's muscles, and awaken also in human breasts an unbounded
devotion to the task.[16]

This is a clear statement of Conrad's reiterated theme – the "idea"'s
dominating the British commercial success in colonial administration. The "idea" is lodged in English administration; the technical
performance is carried out by the Scots colonization. The Scots
nationals residing outside Scotland outnumber the population in
Scotland. They have left their mark all over the East. Calcutta,
the largest industrial center in India, exists as such because of the
Scots engineers who started the city and its organization of jute
mills and factories. In the Orient it is referred to as a "Scots City".
Most all of the shipyards in the East are manned by Scots, and it
is a standing joke that you will never meet an engineer on board a
ship who is not a Scotsman.

In considering the foreign commercial contacts of the United
States with Sulaco and Costaguana through the San Francisco
financier Holroyd, Conrad has plumbed directly to the heart of
the fallacy in our own present-day Foreign Policy. Holroyd wants
to be a silent partner. He states again and again he wants no
responsibility; he merely wants the silver business. Holroyd, as we
seem to do as a culture, leaves not any indication that he has

[14]   *Ibid.*, p. 117.
[15]   *Ibid.*, p. 42.
[16]   *Ibid.*, p. 41.

contributed to Sulaco a particle of the profound qualities of his civilization. In modification, there is in Holroyd a weak and vapid missionary interest to spread a low protestant Christianity, which only suggests itself and comes to nothing. Mrs. Gould answers Charles when he tells her who Holroyd is:

"Ah, yes! The religion of silver and iron. ... My dear Charley, I heard those men talk among themselves. Can it be that they really wish to become, for an immense consideration, drawers of water and hewers of wood to all the countries and nations of the earth?" [17]

Conrad's concise statement sums up what many foreign and national residents of the colonial areas have observed since the end of World War II. In the United States' relations with other countries and nations, with its "aid" to this one and its "aid" to that one, it has tended to contribute nothing but exactly what Holroyd contributes – money. It seems to want in return, their business, all their business – a consideration more "immense" since it asks little else. It is not that to give "aid" is fallacious; but it is the way it is done which condemns it. Funds have been made available by the United States for the most nonsensical projects of any country which bothers to ask. There has been a constant performance of one great swindle after another. The United States apparently gives with no pride, no dignity, no semblance of the "idea". Other countries, particularly in the Orient, stand gaping with astonishment, not only at their phenomenal good luck in this situation, but also at our towering and vulnerable asininity. Our government receives by such giving, such slavish giving, such "drawers-of-water-and-hewers-of-wood" giving, the same repayment James Wait gives the crew – contempt. The aura of contempt surrounds Holroyd in Conrad's presentation. Even more damning – if no contempt is felt, nothing is felt.

In direct contrast to this giving with no contact of any kind between giver and receiver, with no genuine interest, and with no involved effort, is the commercial relationship between Morrison and his villagers. Morrison represents one of the finest natures in

[17]   *Ibid.*, p. 71.

Conrad's work. "Morrison was not only honest. He was honourable, too. . . ." [18]

He was a dearly beloved friend of a quantity of God-forsaken villages up dark creeks and obscure bays, where he traded for "produce". He would often sail through awfully dangerous channels up to some miserable settlement only to find a very hungry population clamorous for rice, and without so much "produce" between them as would have filled Morrison's suit-case. Amid general rejoicings, he would land the rice all the same, explain to the people that it was an advance, that they were in debt to him now; would preach to them energy and industry, and make an elaborate note in a pocket-diary which he always carried; and this would be the end of that transaction. I don't know if Morrison thought so, but the villagers had no doubt whatever about it. . . .

We used to remonstrate with him:

"You will never see any of your advances if you go on like this, Morrison."

He would put on a knowing air.

"I shall squeeze them yet some day – never you fear. And that reminds me" – pulling out his inseparable pocketbook – "there's that so-and-so village. They are pretty well off again; I may just as well squeeze them to begin with."

He would make a ferocious entry in the pocketbook:

Memo: – Squeeze the so-and-so village at the first time of calling.

Then he would stick the pencil back and snap the elastic on with inflexible finality; but he never began the squeezing. [19]

The difference between Holroyd and Morrison, "dearly beloved", lies in the latter's being a provider, not a detached investor; having contact with responsibility, not the unconcern of a "silent partner"; giving because it was needed, not "for an immense consideration". Morrison is "a true humanitarian and rather ascetic than otherwise". [20] He is guilty only "of too much altruism". [21] He is like Lingard, governed by "his straightforward simplicity of motive and honesty of aim". [22]

This English trait of "simplicity of motive and honesty of aim"

[18]   *Victory*, p. 18.
[19]   *Ibid.*, pp. 10-11.
[20]   *Ibid.*, p. 12.
[21]   *Ibid.*, p. 10.
[22]   *An Outcast of the Islands*, p. 13.

as Conrad presents it is certainly not found in the business methods of Dutch Willems:

The quiet deal in opium; the illegal traffic in gunpowder, the great affair of smuggled firearms, the difficult business of the Rajah of Goak. He carried that last through by sheer pluck; he had bearded the savage old ruler in his council room; he had bribed him with a gilt glass coach, which, rumour said, was used as a hen-coop now; he had overpersuaded him; he had bested him in every way. That was the way to get on. He disapproved of the elementary dishonesty that dips the hand in the cash-box, but one could evade the laws and push the principles of trade to their furthest consequences. Some call that cheating. Those are fools, the weak, the contemptible. The wise, the strong, the respected, have no scruples. Where there are scruples there can be no power. On that text he preached often to the young men. It was his doctrine, and he, himself, was a shining example of its truth.[23]

In the matter of inter-relation of native firms and European employees, there is the expected almost general rule that, whereas it is highly honorable for a native to work for a European concern, it is rare for Europeans to take positions with native business houses. In the latter cases it is generally not satisfactory. The methods of conducting trade are too different. A suggestion of this practice is indicated by the fact that Ceylonese estate owners make every effort to engage European estate superintendents and practically refuse to employ Ceylonese in this capacity. It is tacit and expressed knowledge in that country that the European superintendents not only are more efficient but also can be trusted.

There are exceptions.

To serve a Chinese firm is not so bad. Once they become convinced you deal straight by them, their confidence becomes unlimited. You can do no wrong. So Davidson's old Chinaman squeaked hurriedly: "All right, all right, all right. You do what you like, Captain." And there was an end of the matter. . . .[24]

The expression "not so bad" denotes a certain amount of reserve Conrad keeps for this sort of business arrangement. In the short story "Because of the Dollars" he elaborates on his opinion of Chinese businessmen:

[23]   *Ibid.*, p. 8.
[24]   *Victory*, p. 30.

The best of Chinamen as employers is that they have such gentlemanly instincts. Once they become convinced that you are a straight man, they give you their unbounded confidence. You simply can't do wrong, then. And they are pretty quick judges of character, too. Davidson's Chinaman was the first to find out his worth, on some theoretical principle. One day in his counting-house, before several white men he was heard to declare: "Captain Davidson is a good man." And that settled it. After that you couldn't tell if it was Davidson who belonged to the Chinaman or the Chinaman who belonged to Davidson.[25]

It is not only the matters of trust and efficiency which make hiring a European desirable to a native merchant. There is also an ever present quality which proves keen competition for the Malay and Arab traders in Sambir. "Almayer in his quality of white man – as Lingard before him – had somewhat better relations with the upriver tribes." [26]

Interesting to note, this very same quality is exactly what the Arabs do not want when they begin to swing in full tilt their questionable procedure for taking over absolute control of all business. They need commercial assistance. "A white trader would not do. A white man would not fall in with their ideas – would not be trustworthy. The man they wanted should be rich, unscrupulous. ..." [27] Abdulla is their man. The abyss of the betrayer's – of Willems' – weakness and emptiness is made deeper by the fact that he is not even the prime means of the native element effecting their plan.

Willems measured dismally the depths of his degradation. He – a white man, the admired of white men, was held by those miserable savages whose tool he was about to become. He felt for them all the hate of his race, of his morality, of his intelligence. ... [But he is so far gone that] he had, for a moment, a wicked pleasure in the thought that what he had done could not be undone. He had given himself up. He felt proud of it. ... He cared for nothing, for nobody.[28]

The plot succeeded and Almayer's business establishment failed.

He hung on to what little left there was for him in Sambir. In the years that passed, adding to the hopelessness of Almayer's

[25]   "Because of the Dollars", p. 170.
[26]   *Almayer's Folly*, p. 39.
[27]   *An Outcast of the Islands*, p. 57.
[28]   *Ibid.*, pp. 126-127.

degradation, Nina, his daughter, developed into a beautiful young woman and returned to Sambir. Her presence indirectly caused a momentary improvement in Almayer's business position. Rajah Lakamba heard of the beauty of the half-breed girl and thought that it was time, after these many years, to call on the white man. A weak excuse in the form of the purchase of two presentation brass guns ensured the Rajah's "face". He was, however, foiled, since

She was in one of her bad days, and remained in her mother's hut watching with her the ceremonious proceedings on the verandah. The Rajah departed, baffled but courteous, and soon Almayer began to reap the benefit of improved relations with the ruler in the shape of the recovery of some debts, paid to him with many apologies and many a low salaam by debtors till then considered hopelessly insolvent.[29]

This little wave of improvement is augmented by rumors from the outside world of British commercial activity. "The stir made in the whole of the island by the establishment of the British Borneo Company affected even the sluggish flow of the Pantai life. Great changes were expected; annexation was talked of; the Arabs grew civil." [30] British fame was that strong even in a Dutch controlled area. In fact, British commercial reputation, based on more than the idea of pecuniary transactions, was so powerful throughout the Orient that it was used as a standard of judgment by Almayer. During a party for his visiting countrymen, Dutch officials, "Almayer, carried away by his excitement, disclosed his regret at the non-arrival of the English [the British Borneo Company had given up the claim to that part of the East Coast], 'who knew how to develop a rich country', as he expressed it." [31]

[29]   *Almayer's Folly*, p. 32.
[30]   *Ibid.*, p. 33.
[31]   *Ibid.*, p. 36.

VII

THE ETHICAL QUALITIES – ASSUMPTION OF RESPONSIBILITY, COURAGE, AND TRUST – OPERATING IN ANGLO-SAXON COMMERCIAL INTERESTS AND EVERYDAY LIFE IN THE EAST: THE MASTER-SERVANT RELATIONSHIP

Evidence having been presented to indicate Conrad's linking the colonial white man's burden, in the main, to Anglo-Saxons and commercial interests of Anglo-Saxons, we can undertake to examine the ethical qualities involved – assumption of responsibility, courage, trust – and the "burden" 's bearing on everyday life.

Lingard and Lord Jim are the two main characters who portray Conrad's most extensive study in his Eastern books of the ethical qualities. Each man is offered to us on the level of the individual and all that makes him function as an individual, and of a symbol of the principles of British superiority in the East. The Lingard in *The Rescue* well fits a description – not of him – given in the second paragraph of the book:

One of them – a true adventurer in his devotion to his impulse – a man of high mind and of pure heart, lay the foundation of a flourishing state on the ideas of pity and justice. He recognized chivalrously the claims of the conquered; he was a disinterested adventurer, and the reward of his noble instincts is in the veneration with which a strange and faithful race cherish his memory.

Misunderstood and traduced in life, the glory of his achievement has vindicated the purity of his motives.[1]

His entire life is guided by the constant realization of the necessity to take action and to assume responsibility. When Hassim sends that servant of servants, Jaffir, to the unknowing Lingard to warn him away from the danger which will surely result in the death of

[1]   *The Rescue*, p. 4.

Rajah Hassim and his sister, the Princess Immada, Lingard prepares to rescue them:

There was something to be done, and he felt he would have to do it. It was expected of him. The seas expected it; the land expected it. Men also. The story of war and of suffering; Jaffir's display of fidelity, the right of Hassim and his sister, the night, the tempest, the coast under streams of fire – all this made one inspiring manifestation of a life calling to him distinctly for interference. But what appealed to him most was the silent, the complete, unquestioning, and apparently uncurious, trust of these people. They came away from death straight into his arms as it were, and remained in them passive as though there had been no such thing as doubt or hope or desire. This amazing unconcern seemed to put him under a heavy load of obligation.[2]

The same "load" is felt by Captain Mitchell, not unlike Captain MacWhirr in his personality. He explains his assistance and concern in rescuing the ex-Dictator: "Sir, I could do no other. The man was down – ghastly, livid, one mass of scratches." [3] The "load" Charles Gould undertakes is far greater, involving a country, but his reaction is identical: "There were things to be done. We have done them; we have gone on doing them. There is no going back. . . ." [4] Lingard's statement to Jörgenson embodies an old Oriental conception, but his use of the word "share" injects the "idea": "When you save people from death you take a share in their life." [5]

Much later in his history, Lingard continues to show and practice his main characteristic. In a sea-fight with native pirates who attack his ship, he kills almost all of them, including the father of a little native girl. He not only adopts her, provides her maintenance and education, but also secures her a husband. " 'You know I made her an orphan', he often concluded solemnly, when talking about his own affairs. . . ." [6]

However, he never forgets his identity and the incumbent responsibility to his own people. The Travers yacht innocently strands itself directly in the middle of the plans and preparations

[2] *Ibid.*, pp. 87-88.
[3] *Nostromo: A Tale of the Seaboard*, p. 14.
[4] *Ibid.*, p. 207.
[5] *The Rescue*, p. 102.
[6] *Almayer's Folly*, p. 23.

for an Oriental war of succession. It and its passengers become a high point of disturbance to the various factions brought together by Lingard, the key figure in the offensive camps. He could turn his back on its disposal and thereby protect all of the people who had turned to him, as well as prevent the complete collapse of his entire fortune and the plans and activities of over a year. He realizes he is the only person who can help the Yacht and her white people and makes his decision accordingly: "I am a white man inside and out; I won't let inoffensive people – and a woman, too – come to harm if I can help it." [7] Fate has placed him in such a position that he cannot be true at the same time to all the peoples under his influence and guidance; his primary plans and the lives of his main followers – Hassim, the lady Immada, Jörgenson, Tengga, Daman – are all lost. He saves the Yacht and the Traverses; yet he will ever after be "that man who had certainly rescued the white people but seemed to have lost his own soul in the attempt". [8] From his later life in other books we know that the word "seemed" is correct.

Conrad's most objective judgment of him as the British in the East occurs in *An Outcast of the Islands*: "His deep-seated and immovable conviction that only he – he, Lingard – knew what was good for them was characteristic of him, and after all, not so very far wrong. ... His trade brought prosperity to the young State, and fear of his heavy hand secured its internal peace for many years." [9]

Jim is not the positive and virile character that Lingard is, but he is given a more complete analysis by Conrad. There is also a far more deliberate and obvious separation between Jim as an individual person and Jim as an embodiment of the British "idea". As an individual person he has no place in this particular thesis, but there are times when his character as a person merges with his symbolic being. We are told "he was a horrible bungler. Horrible". [10] Every nation bungles certain situations, but none has

[7]   *The Rescue*, p. 39.
[8]   *Ibid.*, p. 453.
[9]   *An Outcast of the Islands*, p. 200.
[10]   *Lord Jim*, p. 155.

the very reputation for it as have the British. Even among themselves the expression "blunder through" is recognized as applicable to their history, and, oddly enough, recognized in a fashion indicative of their tendency to take a pride in shortcomings – as long as they be British shortcomings. Jim's downfalls, anticlimactic and climactic, are caused in the main by the "subtle unsoundness of the man",[11] his inability to be prepared beforehand on short notice to act immediately in a fully conscious manner in time of crisis. As long as he has plenty of time to work mentally a situation as one would work a soft piece of clay, he can then plot his course step by step to a final positive action. If cases arise immediately which require quick positive action – such as the man overboard, the sinking of the *Patna*, the death of Dain Waris – Jim is lost. This, too, this peculiar lack of a particular kind of imagination – not lack of vision – is a British characteristic evidenced in their control of the East. The Sepoy Mutiny of 1857 is probably the best historical example. With hint after hint of the coming revolt apparently everywhere, the situation was ignored until it burst upon the to-be-slaughtered British. Courage was not lacking, but an orderly control of the happening was. In Jim, the trait is excessive. As an individual he is no Hollis [12] as he turns to Marlow after having related his action aboard the *Patna*: "What could I do – what?" [13]

Jim is strongest when he is presented as a symbol:

He was like a figure set up on a pedestal, to represent in his persistent youth the power, and perhaps the virtues, of races that never grow old, that have emerged from the gloom. I don't know why he should always have appeared to me symbolic.[14]

In his colonial exile, "He was protected by his isolation, alone of his own superior kind. . . ." [15] Marlow's last sight of Jim was that of

two half-naked fishermen . . . pouring the plaint of their trifling, miserable, oppressed lives into the ears of the white lord, . . . he was

11 *Ibid.*, p. 89.
12 "Karain: A Memory".
13 *Lord Jim*, p. 84.
14 *Ibid.*, p. 265.
15 *Ibid.*, p. 176.

listening to it, making it his own. . . . Their dark-skinned bodies vanished on the dark background long before I had lost sight of their protector. He was white from head to foot, and remained persistently visible with the strong-hold of the night at his back, the sea at his feet, the opportunity by his side – still veiled. . . . [As Marlow's ship makes way, Jim] appeared . . . a tiny white speck, that seemed to catch all the light left in a darkened world. . . .[16]

In an earlier passage Conrad more openly, but not as poetically, declares Jim's symbolism as British:

I liked his appearance; I knew his appearance; he came from the right place; he was one of us. He stood there for all the parentage of his kind, for men and women by no means clever or amusing, but whose very existence is based upon honest faith, and upon the instinct of courage. I don't mean military courage, or civil courage, or any special kind of courage. I mean just that inborn ability to look temptations straight in the face – a readiness unintellectual enough, goodness knows, but without pose – a power of resistence, don't you see, ungracious if you like, but priceless – an unthinking and blessed stiffness before the outward and inward terrors, before the might of nature, and the seductive corruption of men – backed by a faith invulnerable to the strength of facts, to the contagion of example, to the solicitation of ideas.[17]

Here he writes of "ideas", not the "idea".

Jim's mistake as a young officer, his inability to act instinctively in accordance with the "idea", "drove him away for good from seaports and white men".[18] The fact that he did not unconsciously respond to the dictates of *noblesse oblige* involved in officer-passenger relationship was worse by many a degree since he, a white man, failed the dependent peoples who had placed their trust in him. "At the call of an idea they had left their forests, their clearings, the protection of their rulers, their prosperity, their poverty, the surroundings of their youth and the graves of their fathers. . . . pilgrims of an exacting belief." [19] Because "the men with white faces . . . to that ignorant and pious multitude

---

[16] *Ibid.*, p. 336.
[17] *Ibid.*, p. 43.
[18] *Ibid.*, p. 5.
[19] *Ibid.*, pp. 14-15.

[were] trustworthy",[20] the pilgrims "surrendered to the wisdom of white men and to their courage".[21]

As exacting as was the faith of the Moslem travellers, their confidence in the whites' ability to take them to their destination overbalanced other feelings. The same trust was voiced by the population of Sulaco: "People declared that under the company's care their lives and property were safer on the water than in their own houses on shore." [22] Confidence in the white man was indicated in a more violent case than pure commercial travel and shipping when Hassim fought a hopeless fight against his enemies. "He kept up the struggle, however, with some vague notion that Lingard's arrival would turn the tide." [23] Such dependence became a matter of course in Sulaco:

The fugitive patriots of the defeated party had the knack of turning up again on the coast with half a steamer's load of small arms and ammunition. Such resourcefulness Captain Mitchell considered as perfectly wonderful in view of their utter destitution at the time of flight. He had observed that "they never seemed to have enough change about them to pay for their passage ticket out of the country". And he could speak with knowledge; for on a memorable occasion he had been called upon to save the life of a dictator, together with the lives of a few Sulaco officials – the political chief, the director of customs, and the head of police – belonging to an overturned government.[24]

Not only the natives of the Orient and of South America turn to the Anglo-Saxon for leadership in times of stress. During the revolution in Sulaco, the steamship company's property "and the property of the railway were preserved by the European residents; that is, by Captain Mitchell himself and the staff of engineers building the road, aided by the Italian and Basque workmen who rallied faithfully round their English chiefs".[25] One of Signora Teresa's most bitter complaints against Nostromo is that "he must run at the heels of his English".[26] Her husband displays a different attitude: "Georgio Viola had a great consideration for the English.

[20]   *Ibid.*, p. 85.
[21]   *Ibid.*, p. 17.
[22]   *Nostromo: A Tale of the Seaboard*, p. 10.
[23]   *The Rescue*, p. 82.
[24]   *Nostromo: A Tale of the Seaboard*, p. 11.
[25]   *Ibid.*, p 14.
[26]   *Ibid.*, p. 19.

... Everywhere he had seen Englishmen in the front rank of the army of freedom ... the nation was noble." [27]

Although the ethical qualities in Jim are not as strong in a positive sense as they are in Lingard, Jim is fully aware of the trust in him his assumption of responsibility and white courage have engendered in the people of his land of exile.

"Peaceful here, eh?" he asked. He was not eloquent, but there was a deep meaning in the words that followed. "Look at these houses; there's not one where I am not trusted. Jove! ... Ask any man, woman, or child ... " [28]

Marlow supports this claim to his listeners when describing the constant native intrigue: "Note! Even where he would be most hated he was still trusted." [29]

Jaffir expresses the trust of the East when he says to Lingard, "You are a white man and you can have only one word." [30] His words also reassure himself that he will be treated with no duplicity, a quality quite often present when he deals with his own kind. The natives' faith in Lingard's word is so strong that he is fully justified in saying of its being broken, "They would sooner have expected to see the sun and the moon fall out of the sky. ..." [31] There is no question that his word is broken when his ship fires on the *praus* of the pirates; however, his word is broken not by himself, but by Carter, a young officer left in charge of the *Lightning* who issues the orders to fire not knowing of Lingard's pact that the *praus* shall be left unmolested. This does not change the fact that to the natives the given word in this case was not valid, but it does remove our direct onus from Lingard.

Even the weak Almayer is given trust through his being a European. Dain Maroola says to him during a very important conference, "Who would doubt a white Tuan's word?" [32] This again is not merely Oriental courtesy, but a reflection of the white man's prestige.

---

[27]   *Ibid.*, pp. 30-31.
[28]   *Lord Jim*, pp. 246-247.
[29]   *Ibid.*, p. 249.
[30]   *The Rescue*, p. 333.
[31]   *Ibid.*, p. 328.
[32]   *Almayer's Folly*, p. 53.

When the help of the bandit chief is absolutely essential, the word of Charles Gould – not the silver – is the balance of salvation of Sulaco during the crisis of the revolution. To Gould, Antonia says of the bandit emissary,

It is your character that is the inexhaustible treasure which may save us all yet; your character, Carlos, not your wealth. I entreat you to give this man your word that you will accept any arrangement my uncle may make with their chief. One word. He will want no more.[33]

Antonia's uncle is a South American high government official, but he must have the backing of British Gould to make his word good.

In contrast to the trust placed in all of the above characters, Conrad's own statement about the original Willems' odd position assumes sharper distinction:

My interest was aroused by his dependent position, his strange, dubious status of a mistrusted, disliked, worn-out European living on the reluctant toleration of that Settlement hidden in the heart of the forest-land, up that sombre stream which our ship was the only white men's ship to visit.[34]

There are British qualities other than ethical which have been prominent in obtaining the respect and trust of the natives throughout the East. It is interesting to contemplate the possibility that they may in themselves be the result of that peculiar lack of imagination previously mentioned, the inability to depict what may occur if the routine is broken. This does not detract from their objective value nor from the results they effect. British unconcern is famous everywhere, and may be a key quality in their staunchness. It often approaches excessive stolidity which many times receives the judgment of stupidity – and sometimes is. But its effect among peoples who are famous for excitability is often the creation of a vacuum of inactivity to the end that rash action is prevented, enabling the stolid element to have a better chance of putting its plans into action. When Lord Jim arrived by canoe in an area where the people were not overly anxious to receive strangers hospitably, particularly white strangers, his own

---

[33] *Nostromo: A Tale of the Seaboard*, p. 361.
[34] *An Outcast of the Islands*, p. ix.

boatmen leaped out upon a point of land and raced off. He
jumped out after them instinctively, then turned to face a howling
lot of armed natives heading toward him. He "just stood still and
asked them what was the matter". It is no wonder that "that
seemed to strike them dumb".[35] The same trait served Charles
Gould well in his involvement with the tricky politics of South
America: "His English rock-like quality of character was his best
safeguard. . . ." [36]

In its premeditated form it is an impressive kind of courage.
We are given a good picture of it in Jim and in Marlow when the
latter visits the court of the enemy Rajah with Jim to settle local
complaints:

A rather heavy man, evidently in a position of confidence, with intelligent eyes, a bony, broad, very dark face, and a cheerily officious manner
(I learned later on he was the executioner), presented to us two cups
of coffee on a brass tray, which he took from the hands of an inferior
attendant. "You needn't drink", muttered Jim very rapidly. I didn't
perceive the meaning at first, and only looked at him. He took a good
sip and sat composedly, holding the saucer in his left hand. In a
moment I felt excessively annoyed. "Why the devil", I whispered,
smiling at him amiably, "do you expose me to such a stupid risk?"
I drank, of course, there was nothing for it, while he gave no sign, and
almost immediately afterwards we took our leave. While we were
going down the courtyard to our boat, escorted by the intelligent and
cheery executioner, Jim said he was very sorry. It was the barest
chance, of course. Personally he thought nothing of poison. The remotest chance. He was – he assured me – considered to be infinitely
more useful than dangerous, and so . . . "But the Rajah is afraid of
you abominably. Anybody can see that," I argued, with, I own, a
certain peevishness, and all the time watching anxiously for the first
twist of some sort of ghastly colic. I was awfully disgusted. "If I am
to do any good here and preserve my position", he said, taking his
seat by my side in the boat, "I must stand the risk: I take it once every
month, at least. Many people trust me to do that – for them. Afraid
of me! That's just it. Most likely he is afraid of me because I am not
afraid of his coffee." [37]

Such unruffled courage gives a pragmatic character to a quality
well-known in the Orient – patience. The East is justifiably

35   *Lord Jim*, p. 245.
36   *Nostromo: A Tale of the Seaboard*, p. 86.
37   *Lord Jim*, pp. 250-251.

famous for its practice of patience. Generations will work to create a single art object, to stunt a tree. Long range patience in planning and effecting conquest includes programming beyond the life span of the planners. When they say five hundred or a thousand years, Orientals mean five hundred or a thousand years. The patience of long and unhurried contemplation is the basis for much mystic Oriental philosophy. But patience in attaining altruistic ends of a pragmatic nature does not seem to be part of the practice of the East; and an application of a quality inherent in them, in an unfamiliar manner impresses them. Jim's fortitude has in it the enigma of a positive and active resignation and acceptance which is not quite comprehensible to the Rajah, particularly since it is for the good of others.

Jim's persistent courage was so incomprehensible to Sherif Ali that he dismissed it, to his great regret. When open warfare was the final recourse between Jim's contingent and Sherif Ali, Jim saw a chance of victory in firing cannon from a high mountain top down onto the Sherif's camp. By agonizing effort he dragged and pushed cannon to the top of the difficult peak. The feat seemed so impossible that the Sherif thought Jim mad and paid no attention to his operations. Jim was successful. He told Marlow about it later:

Nobody believed it could be done. Why! I think the very chaps who pulled and shoved and sweated over it did not believe it could be done! Upon my word I don't think they did. . . .[38]

There is excellent contrast in this incident. Jim as an Englishman was able to keep up a positive belief in a seemingly impossible project, while the natives were able to slave physically almost to the point of death on an endeavor they could not accept as feasible. Neither could have changed places with the other. The situation resembles Karain's turning to white "unbelievers" to solve the problems of his own belief. However, although the people were unable to believe in the act, they believed wholeheartedly in Jim:

He was bound to get to the top of that hill and stay there, whatever

[38]   *Ibid.*, p. 264.

might happen. There could be no going back for him. Those people had trusted him implicitly. Him alone! His bare word. . . .[39]

His success by perseverance was not attributed to that quality, but to the man – to the white man. "As to the simple folk of outlying villages, they believed and said (as the most natural thing in the world) that Jim had carried the guns up the hill on his back – two at a time." [40]

This perseverance intensifies the burdening dependence upon the word, the administration of the white man. Since it is the nature of the Anglo-Saxon to apply the quality to almost all endeavors, it is an exhausting demand when involving the every day minutiae of native life. In Jim's case,

They got into the habit of taking his word for anything and everything. . . . Only the other day an old fool he had never seen in his life came from some village miles away to find out if he should divorce his wife. Fact. Solemn word. That's the sort of thing. . . . He wouldn't have believed it. . . . Squatted on the verandah chewing betel-nut, sighing and spitting all over the place for more than an hour, and as glum as an undertaker before he came out with that dashed conundrum. That's the kind of thing that isn't so funny as it looks. What was a fellow to say? – Good wife? – Yes. Good wife – old though; started a confounded long story about some brass pots. Been living together for fifteen years – twenty years – could not tell. A long, long time. Good wife. Beat her a little – not much – just a little, when she was young. Had to – for the sake of his honour. Suddenly in her old age she goes and lends three brass pots to her sister's son's wife, and begins to abuse him every day in a loud voice. His enemies jeered at him; his face was utterly blackened. Pots totally lost. Awfully cut up about it. Impossible to fathom a story like that; told him to go home, and promised to come along myself and settle it all. It's all very well to grin, but it was the dashedest nuisance! A day's journey through the forest, another day lost in coaxing a lot of silly villagers to get at the rights of the affair. There was the making of a sanguinary shindy in the thing. Every bally idiot took sides with one family or the other, and one half of the village was ready to go for the other half with anything that came handy. Honour bright! No joke! – Instead of attending to their bally crops. Got him the infernal pots back of course – and pacified all hands. No trouble to settle it. Of course not. Could settle the deadliest quarrel in the country by

[39]   *Ibid.*, p. 268.
[40]   *Ibid.*, p. 266.

crooking his little finger. The trouble was to get at the truth of anything. Was not sure to this day whether he had been fair to all parties.
It worried him. And the talk! Jove! There didn't seem to be any head
or tail to it. Rather storm a twenty-foot-high old stockade any day.
Much! Child's play to that other job. Wouldn't take so long either.
Well, yes; a funny set out, upon the whole – the fool looked old
enough to be his grandfather. But from another point of view it was
no joke. His word decided everything – ever since the smashing of
Sherif Ali. "An awful responsibility", he repeated. "No, really – joking
apart, had it been three lives instead of three rotten brass pots it would
have been the same. . . ." [41]

The same attitude exists today in the people of the Orient. It may
not be the case of a man from some jungle village – but it can be
if the site is an upcountry installation belonging to a modern oil,
rubber, tea or manufacturing corporation. In the modern cities it
is the filing clerk who cannot afford medicine – a requirement
one must supply in his position of white man. It is the stenographer who has become hopelessly involved with a ruthless money-
lender – an entanglement one must solve if any work is to be
realized from the stenographer. It is the typist who wants to buy
an expensive wedding ring – a request the white must turn down
unless he is willing to ruin himself financially since there is never
any hesitancy about asking. And not only once! It all takes up a
major part of the day. As Conrad writes, "The trouble [is] to
get at the truth of anything." Lingard makes this clear when he
tells Babalatchi, "I am like other whites, and do not wish to
speak many words when the truth is short." [42] Unlike the Western
attempt generally to come straight to a solution as efficiently as
possible, the Eastern approach is to repeat, elaborate, involve,
talk, talk, and talk:

It is but becoming that weighty negotiations should be spread over
many days, that the same requests and arguments should be repeated
in the same words, at many successive interviews, and receive the
same evasive answers. Matters of state demand the dignity of such a
procedure as if time itself had to wait on the power and wisdom of
rulers. Such are the proceedings of embassies and the dignified patience of envoys.[43]

[41] *Ibid.*, pp. 268-269.
[42] *An Outcast of the Islands*, p. 222.
[43] *The Rescue*, p. 373.

The demand is constant. The natives cannot turn to their own, and the whites are few in number. Jim is surrounded by it. There is always someone to approach him:

Their heads were bound in dirty but carefully folded handkerchiefs, and the old man began at once to state a complaint, voluble, stretching a lank arm, screwing up at Jim his old bleared eyes confidently. The Rajah's people would not leave them alone; there had been some trouble about at lot of turtle eggs his people had collected on the islets there. . . .[44]

The concern covers every phase of life! "As to Mrs. Gould, she thinks of her schools, of her hospitals, of the mothers with the young babies, of every sick old man in the three villages." [45] The *serang* aboard the *Lightning* signifies the East's constant and willing awaiting instruction from the West: "Haji Wasub was on deck and ready to carry out the white man's commands." [46] In business life, the guiding control follows the same pattern as we hear the "continuous clink of silver guilders which other discreet Chinamen were counting and piling up under the supervision of Mr. Vinck, the cashier. . . ." [47]

In addition to unconcern, courage, and perseverance, the trait of restraint has built British prestige in the East. This quality among Orientals is a practice of courtesy and may be said to be no inborn phase of the Eastern character. In the British it is natural and not courtesy. In telling about Hassim, his friend for whom he ruined himself, Lingard would exclaim, " 'My word! I couldn't help liking the chap'. . . . This was accepted not as the expression of a feeling, but as the highest commendation he could give his Malay friend." [48] Stein, the great merchant adventurer, always alluded to his very good friend, the Malay sultan he advised and whose sister he married, as "my poor Mohammed Bonso".[49] The somewhat insufferable superior attitude in both

---

[44]   *Lord Jim*, pp. 332-333.
[45]   *Nostromo: A Tale of the Seaboard*, p. 189.
[46]   *The Rescue*, pp. 26-27.
[47]   *Almayer's Folly*, p. 6.
[48]   *The Rescue*, p. 78.
[49]   *Lord Jim*, p. 203.

cases might be considered legitimate since it is an ingenuous recognition, as Conrad presents them, of the true situations.

The relationship between Jim and Dain Waris, because of its artistic importance in the plot of the story, is treated more fully than its prototype between Stein and his "poor Mohammed Bonso". "Theirs was one of those strange, profound, rare friendships between brown and white, in which the very difference of race seems to draw two human beings closer by some mystic element of sympathy." [50] Each was orthodox within his own heritage, as well as a strong individualist. Dain Waris "was of a silent disposition; a firm glance, an ironic smile, a courteous deliberation of manner seemed to hint at great reserves of intelligence and power. Such beings open to the Western eye, so often concerned with mere surfaces, the hidden possibilities of races and lands over which hangs the mystery of unrecorded ages." [51] But the dependence on and worship of the white by his own people was there to overwhelm him. As good as Dain Waris was – strong, courageous, intelligent, having a European mind – "he had not Jim's racial prestige. . . . Beloved, trusted, and admired as he was, he was still one of *them*, while Jim was one of *us*." [52] The prejudice was so great that in time of crisis, instead of meeting at the court of Dain Waris, if Jim happened to be away, "the chief men of the town . . . elected to assemble in Jim's fort for deliberation upon the emergency, as if expecting to find wisdom and courage in the dwelling of the absent white man".[53] In Conrad, the question appears to come back again and again to bare physical courage as a white attribute. Davidson, having only his native crew, is left in a critical predicament when faced with the certainty of battle with rogue whites: "His pacific Kalashes were not to be thought of as against white men." [54] Lingard's mad charge with only a crooked stick brings it about that the "mass of black bodies and frizzly heads in front of him wavered and broke up".[55]

[50]   *Ibid.*, p. 261.
[51]   *Ibid.*, p. 262.
[52]   *Ibid.*, p. 361.
[53]   *Idem.*
[54]   "Because of the Dollars", p. 195.
[55]   *The Rescue*, p. 71.

Conrad also explains the reverence of the East for the white man by concrete evidence of material benefits in addition to the value of the rather abstract qualities of Anglo-Saxon character listed above. All of these qualities can be found in other peoples, but we must keep in mind that the pervading concept of the "idea" defines the characteristics as Anglo-Saxon. In order that the following few passages will not lose some of their power by seeming to be overly unbalanced in stress, I take this opportunity to mention that the not as much negative aspect of white superiority, as reluctant aspect in Conrad's works is offered in the last chapter of this study. Although the concept is quite plainly stated by Jim about Patusan (". . . had I been wiped out it is this place that would have been the loser"),[56] the most detailed treatment of benefits to dependent lands is given in *Nostromo*.

Under the Gould administration, protection extends to the very peasant, an item exploited or ignored by its own kind.

A peaceable Cholo wearing these colours (unusual in Costaguana) [the white and green adopted by the San Tomé mine] was somehow very seldom beaten to within an inch of his life on a charge of disrespect to the town police; neither ran he much risk of being suddenly lassoed on the road by a recruiting party of lanceros – a method of voluntary enlistment looked upon as almost legal in the Republic.[57]

From the beginning of the project "the steadying effect of the San Tomé mine upon the life of that remote province" is felt.[58]

For the San Tomé mine was to become an institution, a rallying point for everything in the province that needed order and stability to live. Security seemed to flow upon this land from the mountain-gorge.[59]

The public bodies of government come to turn to the Gould concession for "the support of the most stable, the most effective force they had ever known to exist in their province".[60] Finally, its influence is great enough to create a new state, for "Sulaco without the concession was nothing".[61] The few Europeans of Sulaco, though not directly connected with the Gould mine, are

[56]   *Lord Jim*, p. 245.
[57]   *Nostromo: A Tale of the Seaboard*, p. 97.
[58]   *Ibid.*, p. 95.
[59]   *Ibid.*, p. 110.
[60]   *Ibid.*, p. 368.
[61]   *Ibid.*, p. 477.

always thought of in their indirect association with it. It guided their activities during the chaotic time of the revolution. "Their last concerted action . . . ended the three days of danger, during which . . . their energy has preserved the town from the calamities of popular disorder." [62] They are able to accomplish this, though small in number, because of their willingness to lead and the others' willingness to follow. The native judgment of Gould, the central figure in spirit, states:

You have proved yourself a just man. There has been no wrong done to any one since you called upon the people to work in the mountains. My brother says that no official of the Government, no oppressor of the Campo, has been seen on your side of the stream. Your own officials do not oppress the people in the gorge. Doubtless they are afraid of your severity. You are a just man and a powerful one. . . .[63]

Charles Gould is one of the very few who are able to be true to others, to their own, and to themselves.

Jim's downfall is an intricately complex matter, but we can say here that it is brought about by the failure of his word, his trust. However, as in the case of Lingard, Jim's trust is broken by another, not by himself. Brown's sneaky, despicable, and cowardly attack on a sleeping camp kills Dain Waris, only son of the powerful chief, old Doramin. The telling fact is that Brown has received from Jim his release which puts him in a position to kill Dain Waris. The combination of Jim's intrinsic slowness of mind, naiveté, and steadfast identity causes him to become a victim of Brown's talk: "You have been white once, for all your tall talk of this being your own people and you being one with them." [64] Jim is unable to see through to the baseness of the man and can react only in the direction of being true to his own kind and his own uncomplicated instincts. The winning blow is Brown's "subtle reference to their common blood".[65] Magnificent power is created in this situation: by the background of benefits to Patusan which Jim has bestowed; by his succumbing to a call which he was confident had no power over him, and which was the very thing

[62] *Ibid.*, p. 307.
[63] *Ibid.*, p. 357.
[64] *Lord Jim*, p. 381.
[65] *Ibid.*, p. 387.

creating above all else at all times in those people who were
dependent upon him a fear expressed in Jewel's unspoken wonder
". . . what would become of her if he should return to these inconceivable regions that seemed always to claim back their
own?",[66] and in Doramin's ponderous anxiety:

The land remains where God had put it; but white men . . . come to us
and in a little while they go. They go away. Those they leave behind
do not know when to look for their return.[67]

And finally, because of the hopelessly resigned desperation which
sets in as soon as Jim's power is broken by his indirect betrayal
of the native people:

. . . there would be no refuge in the land for anyone. A sense of utter
insecurity as during an earthquake pervaded the minds of men, who
whispered their suspicions, looking at each other as if in the presence
of some awful portent.[68]

One of the most astonishing aspects of the relationship between
the white men and the dependent peoples in the Orient is that a
dependence exists in spite of the unfathomably deep difference
between the two groups. The two minds, Eastern and Western, are
different to the point that no full comprehension of one by the
other is possible at any time. It is always a conscious surprise
when one considers that in such a situation one is willing to
administer, and the other is able to prosper under such administration and often turns voluntarily and instinctively to that administration. Conrad's works are full of the realization of the
difference, as are those of many authors who know and deal with
the East. The keynote is struck when Marlow tells Jim, "My
dear chap, . . . you shall always remain for them an insoluble
mystery." [69] At his first arrival in the land, he was not understood
and was found by the natives to be discomposing: ". . . his insistence was alarming; his generosity more than suspicious." [70] His
Anglo-Saxon ingenuousness and lack of ulterior purpose in his
openhandedness did not fit into their scheme of understanding.

[66]   *Ibid.*, p. 308.
[67]   *Ibid.*, p. 274.
[68]   *Ibid.*, p. 410.
[69]   *Ibid.*, p. 306.
[70]   *Ibid.*, p. 243.

Jewel's lack of comprehension of Jim's driving motive is her greatest torment, and results in her greatest unhappiness. When he is being his truest to his abstract ideals, she, in all the sincerity of ignorance, accuses him of being false. After she quietly tells Marlow that Jim has left her, since he deliberately chose death and did not let her die with him, she states, "You always leave us – for your own ends . . . Ah! you are hard, treacherous, without truth, without compassion. What makes you so wicked? Or is it that you are all mad?" [71]

In each case of being "hard", "treacherous", "without truth", "without compassion", Jim is acting in the direct opposite to Jewel's evaluation. Her final question is a judgment by the East on the white man. To them we are all mad. In Jewel's case the profound difference is well brought out in that we cannot fully understand her not understanding Jim, since she comes, in part, of a people who have a philosophy renowned in mystic and fatalistic insight into the abstract.

Cleverness in duplicity is not restricted to any one people; but the Anglo-Saxon in the East has never been particularly successful in this line of endeavor, whereas the Oriental displays a craft so astute and involved that at times it makes a white man feel like an idiot. It is not only the planning and execution of such schemes which mark the difference; the amoral attitude toward such action is even more foreign to the Anglo-Saxons. Lakamba detests Dain Maroola and would like to see him dead, but the following is his accepted plan presented by Babalatchi when the Dutch appear to capture Dain Maroola to hang him:

"There is one of our praus at the southern mouth of the river. The Dutch warship is to the northward watching the main entrance. I shall send Dain off tonight in a canoe, by the hidden channels, on board the prau. His father is a great prince, and shall hear of our generosity. Let the prau take him to Ampanam. Your glory shall be great, and your reward in powerful friendship. Almayer will no doubt deliver the dead body [a prearranged corpse mangled beyond recognition as part of another intricately prepared plan] as Dain's to the officers, and the foolish white men shall say, 'This is very good; let there be peace.' And the trouble shall be removed from your heart, Rajah."

[71] *Ibid.*, p. 348.

"True! True!" said Lakamba.

"And this being accomplished by me who am your slave, you shall reward with a generous hand. That I know!" [72]

After a fight with villagers in which one of his crew is killed and the natives are driven into the jungle, Lingard's attitude makes no sense to Hassim. Hassim, himself a fine man and noble leader, asks Lingard, " 'Will you burn the village for vengeance?' . . . Lingard hesitated. 'No', he said at last. 'It would do good to no one.' " [73] Hassim makes known his surprise. Lingard tells him he will assume responsibility for any woman or child belonging to the dead Lascar. Hassim replies, "O you white men! O the valour of you white men!" [74]

Lingard is even further outside the ring of comprehension of Babalatchi, who addresses Lingard soon after the death of Aïssa's father, an old pirate chieftan:

"Had you come a day sooner, Tuan, you would have seen an enemy die. You would have seen him die poor, blind, unhappy – with no son to dig his grave and speak of his wisdom and courage. Yes; you would have seen the man that fought you in Carimata many years ago, die alone – but for one friend. A great sight to you!"

"Not to me", answered Lingard. "I did not even remember him till you spoke his name just now. You do not understand us. We fight, we vanquish – and we forget." [75]

Babalatchi honestly believes that Lingard has come to kill Willems in stealthy ambuscade, and does everything to further this plan that exists only in his own mind. He forgets himself when discussing Willems. He is brought back to realization of his position when Lingard says,

"It seems that you are angry, O Babalatchi!"

"No; I am not angry, Tuan", answered Babalatchi, descending from the insecure heights of his indignation into the insincere depths of safe humility. . . . "What am I, to be angry with a white man? What is anger without the power to strike? But you whites have taken all; the land, the sea, and the power to strike!" [76]

[72]   *Almayer's Folly*, p. 130.
[73]   *The Rescue*, p. 73.
[74]   *Idem.*
[75]   *An Outcast of the Islands*, p. 227.
[76]   *Ibid.*, p. 229.

Above all, Babalatchi resents because he does not understand "white man's justice; [the] great justice that knows not anger".[77] The vague sense of disconcertion one feels to exist in Babalatchi may be due to the variance between his convictions and existing facts he cannot ignore or refuse to recognize.

"I know the white men, Tuan", he said. . . . "Let one white man destroy another. The will of the Most High is that they should be fools. They know how to keep faith with their enemies, but towards each other they know only deception. Hai! I have seen! I have seen!"[78]

Yet he realizes that these "fools" have been able to take "the land, the sea, and the power to strike".

Another aspect of the unrest in Babalatchi's being is his positiveness of character which causes him to meet restraint everywhere he turns, since he is engaged in action and active pursuits:

He was brave and bloodthirsty without any affection, and he hated the white men who interfered with the manly pursuits of throat-cutting, kidnapping, slave-dealing, and fire-raising, that were the only possible occupation for a true man of the sea.[79]

He has our reluctant admiration and we feel a restricted amount of pity for his sad statement, "They [white men] are very strong. When we fight with them we can only die." [80] Many, many years later, in another book, he reiterates this belief when advising Lakamba, but with a twist of Oriental shrewdness: "White men were strong, but very foolish. It was undesirable to fight them, but deception was easy." And though Babalatchi is sure that "they did not know the use of reason, and he was a match for any of them", Conrad informs us that all this was said with "the confidence of deficient experience".[81]

Deceit is always a legitimate attempt since it is an Oriental trait and the white man is not fully understood – therefore, why not try! To an obvious fabrication, Jörgenson remarked,

"That's a lie!" . . . the shadowy bearer of words preserved a scan-

77 *Idem.*
78 *Ibid.,* p. 60.
79 *Ibid.,* p. 52.
80 *Ibid.,* p. 53.
81 *Almayer's Folly,* p. 84.

dalized silence, though, of course, he had not expected to be believed for a moment. But one could never tell what a white man would believe.[82]

The deficiency of open courage in the Oriental outside of the Japanese area which prevents him – absolutely unarmed – from standing by himself, makes the knife a fitting symbol for his fighting tactics. The difference which exists between the two worlds is aptly brought out by the presentation of the Oriental's attitude toward fighting when Lingard scuffles with Willems for his own good to prevent him from going back into town to seek Hudig:

On the shore end the native caretaker of the wharf watched the combat, squatting behind the safe shelter of some big cases. The next day he informed his friends, with calm satisfaction, that two drunken white men had fought on the jetty. It had been a great fight. They fought without arms, like wild beasts, after the manner of white men. No! nobody was killed, or there would have been trouble and a report to make. How could he know why they fought? White men have no reason when they are like that.[83]

In another section of the same book, we are given the white man's judgment of courage when Conrad writes of the noble Abdulla:

He had never attempted the entrance, however, because men of his race, although brave and adventurous travellers, lack the true seaman-like instincts, and he was afraid of getting wrecked. He could not bear the idea of the Rajah Laut being able to boast that Abdulla bin Selim, like other and lesser men, had also come to grief when trying to wrest his secret from him.[84]

He lacked just that extra bit of courage necessary to enable him to take the chance.

Probably the best example of lack of understanding resulting from the great difference of minds lies in the *serang's* answer to Lingard, who asked the former why he did not tell him there was a boat on the horizon when Shaw, who had not seen it, said there was nothing in sight: "*Malim* [Shaw] spoke. He said: 'Nothing there', while I could see. How could I know what was in his

[82]   *The Rescue,* p. 420.
[83]   *An Outcast of the Islands,* p. 37.
[84]   *Ibid.,* p. 112.

mind or yours, *Tuan*?" [85] Not only did the native not want to dispute the white man's word, but he genuinely believed there might be some reason unknown to him for the false report which was given.

Unable to go native completely enough to understand them and too weak to maintain and retain his own identity, Almayer floats pathetically free between the two worlds, having no intrinsic claim on either. As we consider the fine relationship between Dain Waris and Jim, Lingard and Hassim, Karain and the English Traders, Stein and his "poor Mohammed Bonso", and all the others, we have little sympathy for Almayer's complaint, "the Malays, you understand, are not company for a white man; moreover they are not friendly; they do not understand our ways. Great rascals they are." [86] He becomes more and more obsessed with his white identity as he drifts further and further from it. His sporadic attempts to keep in contact with a white existence impel him to maintain a "big room, opening on the verandah, which he called his sitting-room, whenever, in the company of white men, he wished to assert his claims to the commonplace decencies of civilization. Nobody ever sat there; there was nothing there to sit upon, for Mrs. Almayer in her savage moods, when excited by the reminiscences of the piratical period of her life, had torn off the curtains to make sarongs for the slave-girls, and had burnt the showy furniture piecemeal to cook the family rice." [87]

As long as Almayer kept some idea of identity, "perhaps his white man's pride saved him from that degradation" [88] – sharing Jim-Eng's opium pipe. His shallowness lay in the fact that for gold "he had sacrificed his pride, his honour, and his loyalty . . . by this alliance so distasteful [with Dain Maroola and Lakamba]".[89] Conrad judged his going native as of "a man that fell over a deep precipice and did not die".[90] Nina's judgment was more con-

85   *The Rescue*, pp. 27-28.
86   *Almayer's Folly*, p. 122.
87   *Ibid.*, pp. 90-91.
88   *Ibid.*, pp. 28-29.
89   *Ibid.*, p. 62.
90   *Ibid.*, p. 99.

demning, since she struck to the heart of his lack of identity as she addressed him:

". . . you that cannot be true to your own countrymen. Only a few days ago you were selling the powder of their destruction; now you want to give up to them the man that yesterday you called your friend." [91]

She referred to Dain Maroola, her lover, with whom she then went away. This exposure of something of which he had not even guessed was almost too much for Almayer.

"I cannot", he muttered to himself. After a long pause he spoke again a little lower, but in an unsteady voice, "It would be too great a disgrace. I am a white man." He broke down completely there, and went on tearfully, "I am a white man, and of good family. Very good family", he repeated, weeping bitterly. "It would be a disgrace . . . all over the island, . . . the only white man on the east coast. No, it cannot be . . . white men finding my daughter with this Malay. My daughter!" he cried aloud, with a ring of despair in his voice.[92]

He apparently allowed himself to forget entirely that she was a half-caste, child of a Malay pirate mother, so great was his identifying her being with his white existence. There was only one recourse after that:

. . . only one idea remained clear and definite – not to forgive her; only one vivid desire – to forget her. And this must be made clear to her – and to himself – by frequent repetition. That was his idea of duty to himself – to his race – to his respectable connections; to the whole universe unsettled by and shaken by this frightful catastrophe of his life.[93]

And to forget, he finally turned to that ultimate degradation, Jim-Eng's pipe.

Thus far in this chapter we have seen how the ethical qualities and traits of the Anglo-Saxon and the resultant dependent attitude of the Eastern peoples operate in phases of life – even though every day life – which can be looked upon as somewhat elevated. In the master-servant relationship, with which Conrad concerns himself to a great extent, exists, on a less elevated level, a microcosm of the white man's burden. The relationship is feudal in its

[91] *Ibid.*, p. 181.
[92] *Ibid.*, p. 184.
[93] *Ibid.*, p. 192.

overall aspect, but limited to some extent since the servant is often able to remove himself completely from any responsibility for his acts by tricks and devices known to most European residents in the East. These machinations, it may be commented here, are of similar design and use as those employed at times by many Negro servants in the South of this country. That these tricks work – in that they have no answer which the master, under the system, can allow himself to give – lies in the fact that one accepts from "dependent" servants what one would not accept from white servants. White servant stupidity is not often, as is that of the "dependent" servant, premeditated guile or blatant lying.

Heyst, in a serious situation, is faced with such a problem. After giving Wang the lie-direct about his being sick, Heyst point-blank accuses his servant of stealing the missing revolver:

He had suddenly decided to speak about it, because this frankness could not make the situation much worse than it was. He did not suppose for a moment that Wang had the revolver anywhere about his person; and after having thought the matter over, he had arrived at the conclusion that the Chinaman never meant to use the weapon against him. After a slight start, because the direct charge had taken him unawares, Wang tore open the front of his jacket with a convulsive show of indignation.

"No hab got. Look see!" he mouthed in pretended anger.

He slapped his bare chest violently; he uncovered his very ribs, all astir with the panting of outraged virtue; his smooth stomach heaved with indignation. He started his wide blue breeches flapping about his yellow calves. Heyst watched him quietly.

"I never said you had it on you", he observed, without raising his voice; "but the revolver is gone from where I kept it."

Wang, perceiving that he is losing his assumed position, retreats into the ever ready realm where a white man has no power. " 'Me no savee levolvel', Wang said obstinately." [94] There is nothing short-sighted in the logic of a servant who claims he does not, or did not, understand. No one in the East with a white man's sense of justice can hold a man responsible or punish him for a situation about which he claims absolute incomprehension. It is a powerful shield, and much used.

[94]   *Victory*, p. 312.

The greatest amount of onus for the lack of loyalty between Heyst and Wang lies with the Baron. His refusal to make contact with life and to assume any of the responsibility for the native population expected of a white man, particularly in the case of a servant who is a member of his own household, results in Wang's thinking of him as merely "Number One for whom the Chinaman had neither love nor dislike." [95] Whereas Heyst's detachment is negative, Wang's detachment, in this case, has a positive character that makes it an insult to the unknowing Baron. This is dependent upon the fact that Wang is a Chinaman. That to these people a non-entity is worse than nothing is understandable in the light of their worship of connection. One of the grossest insults you can fling at a Chinaman is to call him a name which translates best into *thing*.

Heyst was unconcerned about Wang and his life. At best he considered him a machine to take care of his house and prepare his food. The fact that Wang asked to stay when all of the Chinese labor was leaving the island after the collapse of the coal company should not have reduced any of the Baron's responsibility for his servant. Heyst's attitude is displayed early in the book when he states as one of the reasons for his not staying at the Netherland House, "they expect you to bring your own servant with you. It's a nuisance".[96] He refuses to conform to this custom which arises out of real necessity. Not only does one's "personal boy", the servant who would accompany his master in traveling, know best how to serve, since he knows his master's habits, but he acts as a barrier to the commercial servants who are at liberty to take full advantage of the people they wait upon. The System of the East demands that your own servant be absolutely loyal to you, but does not make the same demand on commercial (hotel, restaurant, train, barber shop, etc.) servants or on those of other people. For instance, in "Because of the Dollars", when Hollis had finished his tea and paid his bill, "he counted carefully the change handed him by the Chinaman waiter".[97] This small scene is not offered

95   *Ibid.*, p. 307.
96   *Ibid.*, p. 56.
97   "Because of the Dollars", p. 211.

by Conrad to indicate a degree of too much caution or penurious-
ness in Hollis, whom we know to be most generous, but as a
means of setting the scene in a part of the world where inattention
to exact change returned is not a sign of largesse, but a sign of
being a fool and future dupe for any public servant who wishes to
use his prerogative to gain a little extra money under the Eastern
System. Heyst's refusal to take a servant with him was also a
lack of concern for "face", since such a "nuisance" is expected of
white men.

Heyst's cavalier attitude toward keys indicates to the reader as
well as to Wang, that he did not so much trust his servant, as he
did not care. Wang, in concern for his "face", took upon himself
the duty of the ceremony of the keys. In the Orient, the Number
One servant, who is usually also the "personal boy", is given the
household and personal keys. This not only makes him responsible for the house and its contents, but shows that he is trusted
and gives him "face". It is not merely an empty gesture since it
involves the household silver and quite often the personal jewelry
of the family establishment. The keys are, then, both a reality and
a symbol. If a servant feels he is not genuinely trusted as a
"personal boy" or Number One, he will wordlessly present all the
keys to his master. If the master returns the keys to the servant,
all is well and the servant knows his loyalty is still called upon.
Heyst fails in this ceremony, a part of the life he has refused to
engage in, and suffers as a result.

After a time Heyst perceived that Wang had annexed all the keys.
Any key left lying about vanished after Wang had passed that way.
Subsequently some of them – those that did not belong to the store-
rooms and the empty bungalows, and could not be regarded as the
common property of this community of two – were returned to Heyst,
tied in a bunch with a piece of string. He found them one morning
lying by the side of his plate. He had not been inconvenienced by
their absence, because he never locked up anything in the way of
drawers and boxes. Heyst said nothing. Wang also said nothing.[98]

This vacuum relationship, indicative of Heyst's failure, results in
Wang's complete lack of loyalty during a critical period of Heyst's

[98]   *Victory*, p. 180.

attempt to protect Lena and himself. He tells Lena what Wang has said at the barricade of felled trees:

"He told me with horrible Chinese reasonableness that he could not let us pass the barrier, because we should be pursued. He doesn't like fights. He gave me to understand that he would shoot me with my own revolver without any sort of compunction, rather than risk a rude and distasteful contest with the strange barbarians for my sake." [99]

Compare the pleased reception of Renouard, a man strong in the sense of the "burden", by his servant.

"Tse! Tse! The master!" ... Yes, it was the master, the strong master who was never known to raise his voice, the man blindly obeyed and never questioned.[100]

In another case, but indicating the same great trust, Ali, head servant to Almayer, comes to him during a lull in the uprising in Sambir and says, " 'Master, give me the child, there is much trouble in the settlement.' So [Almayer] gave him Nina." [101] He does this without thinking, since he has that much faith in his old servant's devotion. Tamb'Itam's reverence for Jim approached worship:

There was something excessive, almost fanatical, in his devotion to his "white lord". He was inseparable from Jim like a morose shadow. On state occasions he would tread on his master's heels, one hand on the haft of his kriss, keeping the common people at a distance by his truculent brooding glances.[102]

Mr. Jones asks Heyst, "Do you believe in racial superiority, Mr. Heyst? I do, firmly." [103] Jones' servant, the beast Pedro, must also believe in racial superiority since he – voluntarily – abjectly resigns himself to violently brutal beatings by his master after Jones and Ricardo out-wit and capture him. Even under treatment one would not accord to a wild animal, Pedro worships Jones as a god. Probably the only reason Jones does not kill Pedro out-right is that he is subject in a base way to the same "almost un-conscious" feeling Captain Mitchell has for Nostromo. Mitchell

[99]   *Ibid.*, p. 347.
[100]   "The Planter of Malata", p. 61.
[101]   *The Outcast of the Islands*, p. 181.
[102]   *Lord Jim*, p. 270.
[103]   *Victory*, p. 382.

was overcome by the news of the supposed death of Nostromo, in part "because he had become attached to his Capataz as people get attached to their inferiors from love of ease and almost unconscious gratitude".[104]

There is no question of the ease a retinue of devoted servants can bring a man. They also operate as one of the greatest pressure groups for the insistence that the white man maintain his "face". The power of their influence, outside the white man's own pride to maintain his dignity before inferiors, arises from there being so many of them per capita and their being ever present. In the Orient, there are scarcely two minutes in one's non-sleeping hours when a servant is not present. Since they have the backing of the Eastern System they are ruthless in their insistence that their masters maintain "face". They are insufferably snobbish, even though abject.

In a discussion of the unprecedented sight of Schomberg and Zangiacomo rolling on the floor in struggle, the main speaker asked jokingly one of the servants if he climbed a tree to see the fight. "The boy, almond-eyed and impassive, emitted a scornful grunt, finished wiping the table, and withdrew." [105] He was haughty because of the distasteful subject, a servant seeing white men fight, and because of the bad taste displayed by bringing him into the conversation.

"The police *peons* [the lowest form of office messenger-servant] on duty looked disdainfully at the phantom of Captain H. C. Jörgenson" [106] because it was well known that "he was an evident failure".[107] He had gone native. Even though his extensive knowledge was respected, he was not:

Old Jörgenson, gaunt and mute, would turn up at meal times on board any trading vessel in the Roads, and the stewards – Chinamen or mulatos – would sulkily put on an extra plate without waiting for orders.[108]

It was not the extra work which affected the stewards – they like

104   *Nostromo*, p. 344.
105   *Victory*, p. 48.
106   *The Rescue*, p. 98.
107   *Ibid.*, p. 91.
108   *Ibid.*, p. 90.

the importance of extra guests; it was the lack of respect the newcomer commanded.

When Jaffir, court servant of Rajah Hassim and Princess Immada, has swum out to the ship at the risk of his life to save Lingard's, and is asked if there is anything he desires as a reward, he, starving, answers politely,

"A drink of water and a handful of rice for strength to reach the shore. . . . For over there" – he tossed his head – "we had nothing to eat today".

"You shall have it – give it to you with my own hands", muttered Lingard.

He did so, and thus lowered himself in Jaffir's estimation for a time.[109]

Such abasement is accepted as no compliment by the East. Princess Immada is wiser.

The lady Immada, accustomed to the hardships that are the lot of exiles, preferred to walk, but from time to time she let herself be carried for a short distance out of regard for the feelings of her attendants.[110]

In another instance of servant domination,

Tamb'Itam took the paddle from Jim's hand, it being unseemly that he should sit while his lord paddled. When they reached the other shore his master forbade him to come any farther; but Tamb'Itam did follow him at a distance [because of Jim's impending danger], walking up the slope to Doramin's *campong*.[111]

In pride, Ali is Tamb'Itam's equal. The visit of the Dutch naval officers to Almayer causes Ali great concern.

Behind them Ali moved noiselessly laying the table, ranging solemnly the ill-assorted and shabby crockery, the tin spoons, the forks with broken prongs, and the knives with saw-like blades and loose handles. He had almost forgotten how to prepare the table for white men. He felt aggrieved. . . ." [112]

In another book, after saying "Aye, aye, sir" to Lingard,

He strutted towards the landing place thinking proudly that he was

[109]   *Ibid.*, p. 84.
[110]   *Ibid.*, pp. 374-375.
[111]   *Lord Jim*, p. 414.
[112]   *Almayer's Folly*, p. 124.

not like those other ignorant boatmen, and knew how to answer properly the very greatest of white captains.[113]

Almayer asks him of a country native:

"Is Mahmat there?"

"Unless the ill-behaved savage got tired of waiting. Those men know not politeness. They should not be spoken to by white men", said Ali, resentfully.[114]

[113] *An Outcast of the Islands*, p. 279.
[114] *Ibid.*, p. 316.

VIII

THE DEPRESSING ASPECTS OF THE RELATION OF WHITE MAN AND NATIVE WOMAN, AND OF THE HALF-CASTE

In this chapter will be presented depressing aspects of Conrad's colonial *milieu*: the relationship of white man and native woman, and the situation of the half-caste.

Conrad's contrasting Mrs. Travers with Princess Immada falls into line with his belief in white superiority. Although he rarely offers a comparison of the white female and the female of the dependent peoples – in contrast to the great amount of writing in the case of the men – he makes very definite statements in that which he does write:

Fair-haired and white [Mrs. Travers] asserted herself before the girl of olive face and raven locks with the maturity of perfection, with the superiority of the flower over the leaf, of the phrase that contains a thought over the cry that can only express an emotion. Immense spaces and countless centuries stretched between them: and she looked at her as when one looks into one's own heart with absorbed curiosity, with still wonder, with an immense compassion.[1]

The contrast is all the more profound in that Conrad has at every turn presented Immada as a noble and courageous Princess.

Of the two main cases of white men and native women treated in Conrad's stories – Jim's companion was a half-breed – both instances involve the Dutch: Willems and Aïssa, Almayer and the daughter of a pirate chief. (Whether or not there is any conscious or unconscious connection, I will mention the fact that the Dutch have been far less strict about intermixing with the natives than

[1] *The Rescue*, p. 140.

the other large colonial powers, with the possible exception of the French. In the case of the latter it has been convenience; in the case of the former it has been policy. In Conrad's fiction there is a noticeable absence of English involvements – Jim's being the exception – even among the minor characters; Stein and his wife, "The Princess"; Kurtz and his Negress; and Hudig and the half-caste mother of Willems' wife. We must also remember that in the symbolic story of Karain, it is a Dutchman who takes Matara's sister.)

To give ultimate respectability to his daughter, who we know is not the result of an attachment, Lingard "had sworn a mighty oath to marry her to a white man before he went home and to leave her all his money".[2] He chooses the young Almayer as his victim, fully realizing the opposition which must exist to his proposal:

"And don't you kick because you're white!" he shouted, suddenly, not giving the surprised young man the time to say a word. "None of that with me! Nobody will see the colour of your wife's skin. The dollars are too thick for that, I tell you!"[3]

He chose his victim well, for the plan worked; the marriage did not.

Almayer's immediate dreams were of all that the money would do, while "as to the other side of the picture – the companionship for life of a Malay girl, that legacy of a boatful of pirates – there was only within him a confused consciousness of shame that he a white man –"[4] His feelings at the altar were somewhat stronger. "For Almayer was uneasy, a little disgusted, and greatly inclined to run away."[5] The hellish life that followed may have been a bitter disappointment to Mrs. Almayer – "Hai! I! even I, was given in gift by a chief and a warrior to a man that was neither. Hai! Hai!"[6] – but was pure torment to Almayer:

And each of those scenes was concluded by a piercing shriek, reaching him far away. "You know, Kaspar, I am your wife! your own Chris-

[2] *Almayer's Folly*, p. 7.
[3] *Ibid.*, p. 10.
[4] *Idem.*
[5] *Ibid.*, p. 23.
[6] *Ibid.*, p. 148.

tian wife after your own Blanda law!" For she knew that this was the bitterest thing of all; the greatest regret of that man's life.[7]

It was not gold, but towering passion which rushed Willems into the arms of Aïssa. She was attracted to him because "he was of the victorious race".[8] As overwhelming as were his emotions for the girl, they did not completely obliterate his degradation.

Willems never remembered how and when he parted from Aissa. He caught himself drinking the muddy water out of the hollow of his hand. . . . With his returning wits came the fear of something unknown that had taken possession of his heart. . . . His first impulse was that of revolt. He would never go back there. Never! . . . He drank again, and shuddered with a depraved sense of pleasure at the after-taste of slime in the water.[9]

He did go back, but to his agony.

He had a sudden moment of lucidity – of that cruel lucidity that comes once in life to the most benighted. He seemed to see what went on within him, and was horrified at the strange sight. He, a white man whose worst fault till then had been a little want of judgment and too much confidence in the rectitude of his kind! That woman was a complete savage. . . . He tried to tell himself that the thing was of no consequence. It was a vain effort. . . . He seemed to be surrendering to a wild creature the unstained purity of his life, of his race, of his civilization. He had a notion of being lost among shapeless things that were dangerous and ghastly. He struggled with a sense of defeat – lost his footing – fell back into the darkness.[10]

He lost his identity; he was true to no one.

The change in Aïssa was not very attractive, for it was a partial loss of her identity. She dragged Willems before the trussed up Almayer, after the uprising in Sambir:

"'I am like white women', she says, her arms round his neck. You should have seen the faces of the fellows [Almayer's native enemies] in the verandah! They were scandalized and ashamed of themselves to see her behavior. Suddenly she asks him, alluding to me: 'When are you going to kill him?'"[11]

After her alliance with Willems she was unacceptable to her own.

[7]   *Ibid.*, p. 40.
[8]   *An Outcast of the Islands*, p. 75.
[9]   *Ibid.*, pp. 72-73.
[10]   *Ibid.*, pp. 80-81.
[11]   *Ibid.*, p. 184.

When she followed the custom of covering her face in the presence of men, to Willems

She looked like an animated package of cheap cotton goods! It made him furious. She had disguised herself so because a man of her race was near! He told her not to do it, and she did not obey. Would his ideas ever change so as to agree with her own notions of what was becoming, proper and respectable? He was really afraid they would, in time. It seemed to him awful. She would never change! This manifestation of her sense of proprieties was another sign of their hopeless diversity; something like another step downwards for him. She was too different from him. He was so civilized! It struck him suddenly that they had nothing in common – not a thought, not a feeling; he could not make clear to her the simplest motive of any act of his. . . .[12]

His passion and his white identity war within him until they reduce him to wreckage. He hopes that a solution will lie in the removal of Aïssa from her surroundings and her people. He pleads, he rants with her to go away with him:

He did not stop to ask himself whether he could escape, and how, and where. He was carried away by the flood of hate, of disgust, and contempt of a white man for that blood which is not his blood, for that race which is not his race; for the brown skins; for the hearts false like the sea, blacker than night. This feeling of repulsion overmastered his reason in a clear conviction of the impossibility for him to live with her people. He urged her passionately to fly with him because out of all that abhorred crowd he wanted this one woman, but wanted her away from them, away from that race of slaves and cut-throats from which she sprang. . . . And as he spoke his anger and contempt rose, his hate became almost fear. . . .[13]

His passion runs its wild course and thereby leaves him in a state worse than ever before – if we can grasp such an extremity; he hates Aïssa. His identity has now become a hysterical mockery. When his half-breed wife Joanna appears on the scene to beg his forgiveness, he witlessly practically runs in circles attempting to effect some means whereby he can conceal, remove, or hide Aïssa in order "to save his prestige, his superiority".[14] When Lingard condemns him to exile alone with Aïssa, Willems frantically cries out his now false claim to superiority, "I am white! I

[12]   *Ibid.*, p. 128.
[13]   *Ibid.*, p. 152.
[14]   *Ibid.*, p. 352.

swear to you I can't stand this. Take me away. I am white! All white!" [15] The man has become so debased that it is positive relief when Aïssa's devotion undergoes a reversal similar to his. After the scene with Joanna, Aïssa snatches up the fallen revolver and confronts Willems:

Hate filled the world, filled the space between them – the hate of race, the hate of hopeless diversity, the hate of blood; the hate against the man born in the land of lies and evil from which nothing but misfortune comes to those who are not white. And as she stood, maddened, she heard a whisper near her, the whisper of the dead Omar's voice saying in her ear: "Kill! Kill!" [16]

And so she does, with our full approval.

Conrad's attitude toward this topic may be summed up by a little British restraint. It is finely done in his statement about poor, miserable, weak, despicable Bamtz: "One thing, however, must be said of Bamtz; he had always kept clear of native women." [17]

Whereas Conrad expresses a limited sympathy for the native women in the cases of white-brown relations, he expresses very little, if any at all, for the unhappy result of such relationships – the half-caste, or cross-breed. This attitude seems to be unjust since the sad problem is of the white man's own making. It is, in fact, the most distressing aspect of white control in the East – the creation of a group of people rejected by all men, of a group forced to exist in a vacuum in a land demanding orbital connections, a group without any place whatsoever. Their white blood in actuality is a curse, since throughout the Orient it imposes upon them a standard of living their part-bloodedness will not allow them to attain or maintain. They, except the Burghers of Ceylon, are notoriously distrusted by both East and West. Their notoriety in these matters of sneakiness, deceit, and cowardice runs in a vicious circle, causing them to give constant justification for such lack of trust. They are a great pity.

Conrad's lack of sympathy may be due to the fact that he, as a ship's captain, saw them for only short lengths of time. He

[15]   *Ibid.*, p. 271.
[16]   *Ibid.*, p. 359.
[17]   "Because of the Dollars", p. 180.

does not, in his presentation of them as Willems' wife's family, veer from the general attitude of the European and native residents of the East:

They were a numerous and an unclean crowd, living in ruined bamboo houses, surrounded by neglected compounds, on the outskirts of Macassar. He kept them at arm's length and even further off, perhaps, having no illusions as to their worth. They were a half-caste, lazy lot, and he saw them as they were – ragged, lean, unwashed, undersized men of various ages, shuffling about aimlessly in slippers; motionless old women who looked like monstrous bags of pink calico stuffed with shapeless lumps of fat, and deposited askew upon decaying rattan chairs in shady corners of dusty verandahs; young women, slim and yellow, big-eyed, long-haired, moving languidly amongst the dirt and rubbish of their dwellings as if every step they took was going to be their very last. He heard their shrill quarrellings, the squalling of their children, the grunting of their pigs; he smelt the odours of the heaps of garbage in their courtyards: and he was greatly disgusted. But he fed and clothed that shabby multitude; those degenerate descendants of Portuguese conquerers; he was their providence; he kept them singing his praises in the midst of their laziness, of their dirt, of their immense and hopeless squalor; and he was greatly delighted. They wanted much, but he could give them all they wanted without ruining himself. In exchange he had their silent fear, their loquacious love, their noisy veneration. ... His munificence had demoralized them. An easy task.[18]

An excellent picture of the individual crossbreed, and of the astonishing use he makes of the English language as a characteristic of the group, occurs in Marlow's description of the captain of a brigantine. Why the crossbreed's English, called *chi chi* (pronounced chēē chēē), has such a distinctive cast it is hard to say. Its sing-song quality, which is more humorous than lyrical, may result from the influence of the quantitative meter of Oriental languages. Its intensity, which borders on hysterics, may be a pathetic mirroring of an internal franticness of the unidentified individual's trying to assume a sense of belonging in a tight caste society. This attempted assertion may also be the cause of the ridiculous "refinement" of vocabulary and the high pitch of delivery. Conrad's obviously fine ear has enabled him to give an astonishingly accurate representation of *chi chi* English.

[18]   *An Outcast of the Islands*, pp. 4-5.

... her master, a dapper little half-caste of forty or so, in a blue flannel suit, with lively eyes, his round face the colour of lemon-peel, and with a thin little black moustache drooping on each side of his thick, dark lips, came forward smirking. He turned out, notwithstanding his self-satisfied and cheery exterior, to be of a careworn temperament. In answer to a remark of mine (while Jim had gone below for a moment) he said, "Oh, yes. Patusan." He was going to carry the gentleman to the mouth of the river, but would "never ascend". His flowing English seemed to be derived from a dictionary compiled by a lunatic. Had Mr. Stein desired him to "ascend", he would have "reverentially" – (I think he wanted to say respectfully – but devil only knows) – "reverentially made objects for the safety of properties". If disregarded, he would have presented "resignation to quit". Twelve months ago he had made his last voyage there, and though Mr. Cornelius "propitiated many offertories" to Mr. Rajah Allang and the "principal populations", on conditions which made the trade "a snare and ashes in the mouth", yet his ship had been fired upon from the woods by "irresponsive parties" all the way down the river; which causing his crew "from exposure to limb to remain silent in hidings", the brigantine was nearly stranded on a sandbank at the bar, where she "would have been perishable beyond the act of man". The angry disgust at the recollection, the pride of his fluency, to which he turned an attentive ear, struggled for the possession of his broad simple face. He scowled and beamed at me, and watched with satisfaction the undeniable effect of his phraseology. Dark frowns ran swiftly over the placid sea, and the brigantine, with her fore-top sail to the mast and her main-boom amidships, seemed bewildered amongst the cat's-paws. He told me further, gnashing his teeth, that the Rajah was a "laughable hyaena" (can't imagine how he got hold of hyaenas); while somebody else was many times falser than the "weapons of a crocodile". Keeping one eye on the movements of his crew forward, he let loose his volubility – comparing the place to a "cage of beasts made ravenous by long impenitence". I fancy he meant impunity. He had no intention, he cried, to "exhibit himself to be made attached purposefully to robbery". The long-drawn wails, giving the time for the pull of the men catting the anchor, came to an end, and he lowered his voice. "Plenty too much enough of Patusan", he concluded, with energy.

I heard afterwards he had been so indiscreet as to get himself tied up by the neck with a rattan halter to a post planted in the middle of a mud-hole before the Rajah's house. He spent the best part of a day and a whole night in that unwholesome situation, but there is every reason to believe the thing had been meant as a sort of joke. He brooded for a while over that horrid memory, I suppose, and then addressed in a quarrelsome tone the man coming aft to the helm. When he turned to me again it was to speak judicially, without passion. He would take the gentleman to the mouth of the river at Batu Kring (Patusan town "being situated internally," he remarked, "thirty miles"). But in his eyes, he continued – a tone of bored, weary conviction replacing his previous voluble delivery – the gentleman was already "in the similitude of a corpse". "What? What do you say?" I asked. He assumed a startlingly ferocious demeanour, and imitated to perfection the act of stabbing from behind. "Already like the body of one deported", he explained, with the insufferably conceited air of his kind after what they imagine a display of cleverness. . . .

Then, while the half-caste, bursting with importance, shouted his orders, [Marlow takes leave of Jim and departs from the ship.] . . . I could see the little wretch's face, the shape and colour of a ripe pumpkin, poked out somewhere under Jim's elbow. He, too, raised his arm as if for a downward thrust. *Absit omen!* [19]

But it is not.

Cornelius, another filthy half-caste, plays a major role in the betrayal of Jim.

Cornelius broke upon it [Marlow's mood]. He bolted out, vermin-like, from the long grass growing in a depression of the ground. I believe his house was rotting somewhere near by, though I've never seen it, not having been far enough in that direction. He ran towards me upon the path; his feet shod in dirty white shoes, twinkled on the dark earth: he pulled himself up, and began to whine and cringe under a tall stove-pipe hat. His dried-up little carcass was swallowed up, totally lost, in a suit of black broadcloth. That was his costume for holidays and ceremonies, and it reminded me that this was the fourth Sunday I had spent in Patusan. All the time of my stay I had been vaguely aware of his desire to confide in me, if he only could get me all to himself. He hung about with an eager craving look on his sour yellow little face; but his timidity had kept him back as much as my natural reluctance to have anything to do with such an unsavory creature. He would have succeeded, nevertheless, had he not been so ready to slink off as soon as you looked at him. He would slink off before Jim's severe gaze, before my own, which I tried to make indifferent, even before Tamb'Itam's surly, superior glance. He was perpetually slinking away; whenever seen he was seen moving off deviously, his face over his shoulder, with either a mistrustful snarl or a woe-begone, piteous, mute aspect; but no assumed expression could conceal this innate irremediable abjectness of his nature, any

[19] *Lord Jim*, pp. 238-241.

more than an arrangement of clothing can conceal some monstrous deformity of the body. . . .

It was trying; but the contempt, the unreasoned contempt, the man's appearance provoked, made it easier to bear. He couldn't possibly matter.[20]

The Portuguese, being the first Western nation to explore a great part of the Eastern world, laid the foundation for the half-caste groups. From the great number of Portuguese crossbreeds, even considering inbreeding which has occurred within the groups themselves, we can assume that their Portuguese forefathers were rather active in creating an almost new kind of people. This assists in explaining why Conrad so often refers to Portuguese half-castes to the exclusion of the other types. In writing of Davidson's crew aboard the *Sissie*, he states, "the nearest approach to another white man on board of her was the engineer, a Portuguese half-caste, as thin as a lath and quite a youngster at that".[21] Because the Portuguese themselves do not conform to the demands of the "burden", "Morrison refused to accept the racial whiteness of the Portuguese officials".[22]

The secondary European groups clutch at the cloak of respectability which their white blood gives them, in order to gain some cover of the prestige and privileges that accompany the entire costume. The intensity with which the identity is claimed causes the resultant over-refinement of patent-leather boots and absurdity of English usage we have already noticed. In the ridiculous separation scene between Willems and his wife, Joanna, Leonard, her brother, portrays his part in perfect keeping with his identity – or his lack of it:

From under the house, where there were bathrooms and a tool closet, appeared Leonard, a rusty iron bar in his hand. He called threateningly from the bottom of the stairs.

"Do not hurt her, Mr. Willems. You are a savage. Not at all like we, whites."

"You too!" said the bewildered Willems. "I haven't touched her. Is this a mad house?" He moved toward the stairs, and Leonard dropped the bar with a clang and made for the gate of the compound.

[20]   *Ibid.*, pp. 323-324.
[21]   "Because of the Dollars", pp. 172-173.
[22]   *Victory*, p. 13.

... At the gate he [Willems] came suddenly upon Leonard, who had been dodging about there and failed to get out of the way in time.

"Do not be brutal, Mr. Willems", said Leonard, hurriedly, "It is unbecoming between white men with all those natives looking on." Leonard's legs trembled very much, and his voice wavered between high and low tones without any attempt at control on his part. "Restrain your improper violence", he went on mumbling rapidly. "I am a respectable man of a very good family, while you ... it is regrettable ... they all say so. ..."

"What?" thundered Willems. He felt a sudden impulse of mad anger, and before he knew what had happened he was looking at Leonard da Souza rolling in the dust at his feet. He stepped over his prostrate brother-in-law and tore blindly down the street, everybody making way for the frantic white man.[23]

A more serious examination of the position of the half-caste is found in Nina, daughter of Almayer. For her, as for the other female crossbreeds in his works, Conrad allows the reader to experience an unemotional sympathy, as opposed to the complete lack of it permitted the men. Even in his physical description of her he decidedly splits her identity:

Her firm mouth, with the lips slightly parted and disclosing a gleam of white teeth, put a vague suggestion of ferocity into the impatient expression of her features. And yet her dark and perfect eyes had all the tender softness common to Malay women, but with a gleam of superior intelligence; they looked out gravely, wide open and steady, as if facing something invisible to all other eyes. She stood there all in white. ...[24]

He writes again of her eyes, "where the startled expression common to Malay womankind was modified by a thoughtful tinge inherited from her European ancestry".[25]

She is her father's greatest pride and greatest torment as he day-dreams: "They would live in Europe, he and his daughter. They would be rich and respected. Nobody would think of her mixed blood in the presence of her great beauty and of his immense wealth." [26] Conrad shows us when the Dutch naval officers pay Almayer one of their rare visits, how false the dream is with regard to respect and the unconcern for her "mixed blood".

23   *An Outcast of the Islands*, pp. 28-29.
24   *Almayer's Folly*, p. 17.
25   *Ibid.*, p. 29.
26   *Ibid.*, p. 3.

The young sub [-lieutenant] began to recover from the astonishment and confusion caused by Nina's unexpected appearance and great beauty. "She was very beautiful and imposing", he reflected, "but after all a half-caste girl". This thought caused him to pluck up heart and look at Nina sideways.[27]

Captain Ford, who has brought Nina from the Vinck's home in Singapore to Almayer, bluntly explains to him why he had to give her passage to Sambir. " 'You know, Kasper', he said, in conclusion, to the excited Almayer, 'it is deucidly awkward to have a half-caste girl in the house'." [28] Kasper flares up after more details of the situation are given him, until Ford says, "You can't make her white." [29] That is the crux of the entire matter. You can make them native, but you cannot make them white. She never becomes fully native, so that Babalatchi's judgment is typically Eastern. "She told me so herself, speaking to me openly, for she is half white and has no decency. . . . That is what she said, speaking to my face, as I am speaking now to you, Rajah. She is like a white woman and knows no shame." [30] Her native blood crops out in her ready ability to adapt "herself wonderfully to the circumstances of a half savage and miserable life. She accepted without question or apparent disgust the neglect, the decay, the poverty of the household, the absence of furniture, and the preponderance of rice diet on the family table." [31] She is conscious of her in-between existence and seeks for some identity of her own from her savage mother:

And listening to the recital of those savage glories, those barbarous fights and savage feasting, to the story of deeds valorous, albeit somewhat bloodthirsty, where men of her mother's race shone far above the Orang Blanda, she felt herself irresistibly fascinated, and saw with vague surprise the narrow mantle of civilized morality, in which good-meaning people had wrapped her young soul, fall away and leave her shivering and helpless as if on the edge of some deep and unknown abyss. Strangest of all, this abyss did not frighten her when she was under the influence of the witch-like being she called her mother. She seemed to have forgotten in civilized surroundings her life before

27   *Ibid.*, p. 126.
28   *Ibid.*, p. 30.
29   *Ibid.*, p. 31.
30   *Ibid.*, pp. 127-128.
31   *Ibid.*, p. 31.

the time when Lingard had, so to speak, kidnapped her from Brow. Since then she had had Christian teaching, social education, and a good glimpse of civilized life. ... The education ended in a scene of humiliation, in an outburst of contempt from white people for her mixed blood. ... Her young mind having been unskillfully permitted to glance at better things, and then thrown back again into the hopeless quagmire of barbarism, full of strong and uncontrolled passions, had lost the power to discriminate. It seemed to Nina that there was no change and no difference. ... To her resolute nature, however, after all these years, the savage and uncompromising sincerity of purpose shown by her Malay kinsmen seemed at least preferable to the sleek hypocrisy, to the polite disguises, to the virtuous pretences of such white people as she had had the misfortune to come in contact with. After all it was her life; it was going to be her life, and so thinking she fell more and more under the influence of her mother. Seeking, in her ignorance, a better side to that life, she listened with avidity to the old woman's tales of the departed glories of the Rajah, from whose race she had sprung, and she became gradually more indifferent, more contemptuous of the white side of her descent represented by a feeble and traditionless father.[32]

The conflict within her is eternal.

She is never able to become wholly one or the other; but she makes her choice of direction when she breaks out in a rage at the Dutch officers who seek her lover, Dain Maroola:

"And he killed white men!" interrupted Nina.

"I regret to say they were white. Yes, two white men lost their lives through that scoundrel's freak."

"Two only!" exclaimed Nina.

The officer looked at her in amazement.

"Why! Why! you – " he stammered, confused.

"There might have been more", interrupted Nina. "And when you get this – this scoundrel, will you go?"

The lieutenant, still speechless, bowed his assent.

"Then I would get him for you if I had to seek him in a burning fire", she burst out with intense energy. "I hate the sight of your white faces. ... I hoped to live here without seeing any other white face but this", she added in a gentler tone, touching lightly her father's cheek.[33]

Her most courageous and admirable choice is in her rejection of Almayer for Dain Maroola. Her father tells her in desperation,

---

[32]   *Ibid.*, pp. 42-43.
[33]   *Ibid.*, pp. 140-141.

"Between him and you there is a barrier that nothing can remove." [34] She tortures him with the taunt of her hopeless position: "Scorn for scorn, contempt for contempt, hate for hate. I am not of your race. Between your people and me there is also a barrier that nothing can remove. You ask why I want to go, and I ask you why I should stay." [35]

Nina's unusual courage gives her outlook more hope than can be properly predicted for those others in her same position. The more general situation is depicted by the wretched Joanna, wife of Willems, to whom even Ali, a mere servant, refers as "that Sirani woman".[36] Even the protection of this contemptuous detachment is taken away in the reaction of Aïssa to Joanna:

She stood in sudden stillness, looking at Joanna with surprised contempt.

"A Sirani woman!" she said, slowly, in a tone of wonder.

Joanna rushed at Willems – clung to him, shrieking: "Defend me, Peter! Defend me from that woman!"

"Be quiet. There is no danger", muttered Willems, thickly.

Aïssa looked at them with scorn. "God is great! I sit in the dust at your feet", she exclaimed jeeringly, joining her hands above her head in a gesture of mock humility. "Before you I am as nothing." She turned to Willems fiercely, opening her arms wide. "What have you made of me?" she cried, "you lying child of an accursed mother! What have you made of me? The slave of a slave. Don't speak! Your words are worse than the poison of snakes. A Sirani woman. A woman of a people despised by all."

She pointed her finger at Joanna, stepped back, and began to laugh.[37]

[34]   *Ibid.*, p. 178.
[35]   *Ibid.*, p. 179.
[36]   *An Outcast of the Islands*, p. 316.
[37]   *Ibid.*, pp. 357-358.

IX

THE OPPRESSIVE PESSIMISM REALIZED BY
THOSE INDIVIDUALS ACCEPTING THE
RESPONSIBILITY OF THE COLONIAL BURDEN

This chapter organizes certain aspects of Conrad's treatment of
the colonial burden under the general topic of his reluctance in
the accepting of it. As this term is one of those which have shades
of meanings it is impossible to get from a dictionary, the word
"pessimism" might be better used since there is no question that
Conrad does not oppose qualities of heritage in white men, which
they would fail if they did not exercise. Conrad's "reluctance", as
it is used above, implies the resigned acceptance of man's imperfection to comply in all ways with his – in their pure form –
perfect attributes.

Certainly the subject of the half-caste could be included as a
reluctant phase of the "burden", but I have attempted to restrict
this topic to those places in Conrad's fiction where he makes a
more or less definitely outspoken relationship between the situation and the reluctance. The topic will be presented under three
main subdivisions: the oppression on the East which any foreign
administration would necessarily impose, the wretchedness and
miserableness of the attitude of the East itself, and the oppression
as an abstract quality felt by the foreign unofficial administrators
in complying with the demands of their destiny.

Conrad is constantly aware of the intricacy of the problem of
the dependent peoples. In the "Author's Note" to *Almayer's
Folly*, he says, in effect, that they who do not know seem "to
think that in those distant lands all joy is a yell and a war dance,
all pathos is a howl and a ghastly grin of filed teeth, and that the

solution of all problems is found in the barrel of a revolver or on the point of an assegai".[1] I hope that this paper will have brought out to some extent the complexity antipodal to the above.

The trait of courage shown by the Malays arouses Conrad's sympathy to the extent that he is willing to write, "their country . . . has fallen a prey to the Western race – the reward of superior strength if not of superior virtue".[2] There is the suggestion here of more nostalgia for the old days of war-like deeds than hesitancy to believe that a question does not exist concerning the comparative virtues of brown and white. However, later on, Hassim's open doubt focuses our attention on the difference between the professions of and the practices of the purposes in the subjection of the East.

"Your country is very powerful – we know", began again Hassim after a pause, "but is it stronger than the country of the Dutch who steal our land?"

"Stronger?" cried Lingard. He opened a broad palm. "Stronger? We could take them in our hand like this – " and he closed his fingers triumphantly.

"And do you make them pay tribute for their land?" inquired Hassim with eagerness.

"No", answered Lingard in a sobered tone; "This, Tuan Hassim, you see, is not the custom of white men. We could, of course – but it is not the custom."

"Is it not?" said the other with a skeptical smile. "They are stronger than we are and they want tribute from us." [3]

Tengga, though he fulfills his promise of warriors and a prau for Lingard, remarks after thoughtful silence,

"We must not touch them [the Travers and the crew of their yacht] because their skin is like yours and to kill them would be wrong, but at the bidding of you whites we may go and fight with people of our own skin and our own faith – and that is good." [4]

The Chieftan Tengga's argument sounds convincing, but not when we compare the virtue of each side. Tengga would attack the yacht for plunder and the joy of killing the crew. By his code

1   *Almayer's Folly*, p. ix.
2   *The Rescue*, p. 3.
3   *Ibid.*, pp. 75-76.
4   *Ibid.*, p. 173.

this activity is virtuous and quite just; but it does not compare favorably with Lingard's purpose in using the Chieftan's men and prau to re-establish the rightful rulers Hassim and Immada in their land. Tengga completely misjudges Lingard's restrictions based on abstract judgment of right and wrong. The odd fact is that he would have less respect for Lingard if he knew Lingard's basic compulsion in acting as he does. He would think him a fool.

Mr. Travers is a fool. He busies himself sailing about the East "to study the Dutch colonial system. Wants to expose it. . . ." [5] His purpose is admirable, but he is not the man for it. In the crises which arise over his yacht, he, instead of co-operating with Lingard who embodies the better qualities of colonial administration, conducts himself in a doltishly dumb fashion resulting in great trouble for all. He is a good example of the predominant stupidity of officialdom. Daman, another chieftan, asks about the Travers yacht a question both prophetic and to the point:

Why, asked Daman, did these strange whites travel so far from their country? The great white man [Lingard] whom they all knew did not want them. No one wanted them. Evil would follow in their footsteps. They were such men as are sent by rulers to examine the aspects of far-off countries and talk of peace and make treaties. Such is the beginning of great sorrows.[6]

Conrad's distaste for the interference of government agencies appears in the above passage. We have already discussed his great respect for the individuals of the commercial pursuits in the East. In their capacity as administrators over Oriental lives, they do not have the heavy oppressiveness upon liberty which one associates with Governments or States. The commercial individuals are also more dependent upon themselves as they, in their activities, do not have the ponderous power of a State to fall back upon. The British have not been blind to the efficacy of the non-departmentalized Anglo-Saxon, for some of the greatest influences in the East have been exerted by men with no official titles who

5 *Ibid.*, p. 34.
6 *Ibid.*, p. 223.

have been placed with or loaned to Oriental governments merely as advisors. Not the qualities of these men alone have made the plan fortunate; the willingness of the East to turn to the white man has permitted this procedure to operate successfully. The individual does not appear to be absorbing the liberty of those dependent upon him. Conrad's opposition lies in the fact that the Western State does exist as a control in the East.

Conrad's opposition becomes quite ruthless in "The Planter of Malata". The nameless Editor, the "distinguished journalist",[7] holds up to Renouard the "two big F's" [8] as symbols of success in his colonial world, Fashion and Finance. He manages to mention in an off-hand manner at least three different times in a very short while, that he was invited but could not manage to attend a very select dinner party given by a high colonial official.[9] A little past the middle of the story, Renouard, under the impetus of observing the highly placed colonial official, makes his own identification of the two big F's, "Froth and Fraud!" [10]

Conrad's attack against huge, impersonal commercial interests is given us in the person of Willy Dunster, nephew of the highly placed colonial official. "He holds the paper in both hands, hunches his shoulders up to his ugly ears, and brings his long nose and his thick lips onto it like a sucking apparatus. A commercial monster." [11] We may assume that he reads it with his "boiled eyes".[12] Finally, "this large, bilious creature was an economist and a sentimentalist, facile to tears, and a member of the Cobden Club".[13]

The imperfections in the individual are so dominant in Willems and other Dutch whites about whom and with whom Aïssa has heard or come in contact that she voices the cry of the ultra independent's view of the West: "A land of lies and of evil from which nothing but misfortune ever comes to us – who are not

---

[7]   "The Planter of Malata", p. 11.
[8]   *Ibid.*, p. 17.
[9]   *Ibid.*, pp. 4, 8, 13.
[10]   *Ibid.*, p. 45.
[11]   *Ibid.*, p. 4.
[12]   *Ibid.*, p. 24.
[13]   *Ibid.*, p. 33.

white." [14] After the exhausting scene with her father who entreats her to finish the attempt which he failed, to kill Willems, she faces her lover: " 'Nothing but misfortune', she whispered, absently, to herself. 'Nothing but misfortune to us who are not white.' " [15]

In Babalatchi's confused statement lies a kernel of truth which appears profoundly strong when viewed from his, as from Tengga's position, but loses its appeal as one moves out to a more objective site from which to examine it. The sorrow lies in the genuine inability of the "Babalatchies" to see the truth of virtue and happiness in its objective form. For them, therefore, the objective truth may as well not exist:

"If I ever spoke to Patalolo, like an elder brother, it was for your good – for the good of all", said Lingard with great earnestness.

"This is a white man's talk", exclaimed Babalatchi, with bitter exultation. "I know you. That is how you all talk while you load your guns and sharpen your swords; and when you are ready, then to those who are weak you say: 'Obey me and be happy, or die!' You are strange, you white men. You think it is only your wisdom and your virtue and your happiness that are true. ... You are wise and great – and you shall always be fools." [16]

To any one who has lived in the East, Babalatchi's claim to more than one wisdom has much weight, particularly with regard to the question of religion. Conrad's antagonism to Christian missionary exertions is the attitude taken by the general resident Europeans. There are good reasons for such a rejection of missionary zeal, which does not necessarily involve the rejection of Christian theology. The cultures of the Orient are old, complex, civilized, and have been concerned for thousands of years before Christianity with the problem of man's place in the universe and beyond. The Eastern religions are highly developed, mature, and profound – and often more penetratingly philosophical than Christianity. There is then, an element of offensiveness in the situation of Christian missionaries' coming out, often and usually, particularly in the Protestant denominations, poorly educated socially and academically, to areas unlike their own and spreading the word

[14] *An Outcast of the Islands*, p. 144.
[15] *Ibid.*, p. 151.
[16] *Ibid.*, p. 226.

that all are going to hell or are lost if they do not believe as the Christian missionaries do.

Besides the abstract offense of the above, there is the practical and material side of the question. Christian missionaries have often been criticized by both European and national residents for such things as not paying their servants. The missionary reply is that the servants are working for God since the missions are established for God, and that they should not expect pay. Indirectly God may be involved, but the servants are washing the missionaries' laundry, cooking and serving the missionaries' food, cleaning the missionaries' Godly houses, and nursing the missionaries' unGodly children. In a caste society where the servant class are not bright enough to be on a competative basis with the rest of the social order, to all but the missionaries, the missionary approach seems somewhat unethical.

In addition, the practical matter of converts must be dealt with. The majority of converts come from the lower castes; and too often, the acceptance of Christianity is looked upon as a release from the restrictions ethical and practical of their former castes more than the assumption of Christian theology. Many Europeans and practically all nationals avoid hiring Christian converts, particularly as servants, since they are much given to the Christian practices, if not doctrines, of cheating, lying, and stealing.

Marlow's comment on missionary work is given to us in the mass of inefficiency he discovers in *Heart of Darkness*.

I appeared, however, I was also one of the Workers, with a capital — you know. Something like an emissary of light, something like a lower sort of apostle. There had been a lot of such rot let loose in print and talk just about that time, and the excellent woman [Marlow's aunt], living right in the rush of all that humbug, got carried off her feet. She talked about "weaning those ignorant millions from their horrid ways", till, upon my word she made me quite uncomfortable.[17]

A stronger and more penetrating comment of missionary zeal and offensiveness is offered in the scene of the cook's trying to "save" Jimmy, the "nigger" of the *Narcissus*. The cook's "heart overflowed . . . with the desire to meddle, with anxiety for the soul of

[17]   *Heart of Darkness*, p. 59.

that black man. . . . Snatch him up in his arms and pitch him right into the middle of salvation. . . . The black soul – blacker – body – rot – Devil. No! Talk – strength – Sampson. . . ." [18] And so he raves on "through the infernal fog of his supreme conceit. . . . The cook's lips moved without a sound; his face was rapt, his eyes turned up. He seemed to be mentally imploring deck beams, the brass hook of the lamp, two cockroaches . . . . The cockroaches ran away." [19] Conrad has made clear by these passages his antagonism to the attack on basic themes and strains of other cultures. It is again the question of identity and recognition of different philosophies for different peoples, and the opposition to throat-cramming procedures to obtain acceptance of one group's view by others. The casual, civilized, cultivated exchange of ideas and concepts, beliefs and convictions, as offered in the conversation between Karain and the traders, is permissible and desirable since it engenders better appreciation by both parties; but not permissible is that disgusting and sickening hammering-in method of those "Workers" with a "message". Here is unbalance and cosmic rudeness: the assuming an overall superiority in a phase of life where it does not exist. This modern crusading is comparable on an intellectual level to the carcass of a middle-aged Negro with a bullet-hole in his forehead being, according to Marlow's cynical comment, considered "as a permanent improvement" by the Belgian administration.[20]

To return to Babalatchi's accusation, at this point let us examine, as Conrad offers it, the "virtue" of the East for which Babalatchi claims an equal truth. We can refute this claim; but we cannot refute his claim that white men "shall always be fools". In this he is correct, since he means that we will never fully understand the Oriental.

Although Jim is fully justified in understating, "I've done a thing or two for them",[21] he "was to be murdered mainly on religious grounds. . . . A simple act of piety (and so far infinitely

---

18   *The Nigger of the Narcissus*, p. 115.
19   *Ibid.*, p. 116.
20   *Heart of Darkness*, p. 71.
21   *Lord Jim*, p. 306.

meritorious), but otherwise without much importance".[22] There is not even the natural act of piety with regard to Almayer, "the white man, whom they trusted and liked, and called a fool amongst themselves".[23] In his case murder was a matter of casual convenience.

"Almayer must die", said Lakamba, decisively, "to make our secret safe. He must die quietly, Babalatchi. You must do it."

Babalatchi assented, and rose wearily to his feet. "Tomorrow?" he asked.

"Yes; before the Dutch come. He drinks much coffee", answered Lakamba, with seeming irrelevancy.[24]

As foreign to our sense of "virtue" as this merciless unconcern for human life is, it assumes a revulsion-inspiring depravity of cruelty when considered in the light of the East's attitude toward the East. One of the most puzzling and amazing facets of Oriental cultures is the delight the members apparently take in mistreating each other. This trait is so pronounced in India that even the nationals agree to a saying that "an Indian would rather mistreat another Indian than a European". Quite often a European walking down a street in Calcutta, years after Indian independence, could have the experience of one Indian violently shoving another Indian to make way for the white man. It is not done out of excessive concern for the European, but out of pure delight in lording it over another national. When an Indian driving a car deliberately knocks down a national pedestrian, with no great physical harm resulting, the passers-by react with hoots of derision and delight at the sprawled pedestrian. A mild example is given in Mr. Juke's account of MacWhirr's dividing the Chinamen's gold:

As to giving up the money to any Chinese official he could scare up in Fu-chau, he said he might just as well put the lot in his own pocket at once for all the good it would be to them. I suppose they thought so, too.[25]

"These Chinamen know their officials better than we do." [26]

22   *Ibid.*, p. 310.
23   *Almayer's Folly*, p. 197.
24   *Ibid.*, p. 88.
25   *Typhoon*, pp. 101-102.
26   *Ibid.*, p. 100.

Even the objective gorge rises high at Makola, the Negro station clerk in "An Outpost of Progress", as he cleverly manipulates a trade with wandering slave hunters for a few tusks of ivory – his wares of the moment being his own Negro compound laborers! Does this infamy shock the Negro laborers? Absolutely not! The shock is reserved for us; they expect such treatment.

Belonging to a tribe from a very distant part of this land of darkness and sorrow, they did not run away, naturally supposing that as wandering strangers they would be killed by the inhabitants of the country; in which they were right.[27]

Such disturbing indifference is not as pronounced in other areas of Conrad's concern as it is in Africa. The same oppression under their own rule exists for the people of Sulaco, but they do complain: "And on all the lips she [Mrs. Gould] found a weary desire for peace, the dread of officialdom with its nightmarish parody of administration without law, without security, and without justice." [28] They complain. And that is all they do. They show no other reaction.

This gossip of the inland Campo, so characteristic of the rulers of the country with its story of oppression, inefficiency, fatuous methods, treachery, and savage brutality, was perfectly known to Mrs. Gould. That it should be accepted with no indignant comment by people of intelligence, refinement, and character as something inherent in the nature of things was one of the symptoms of degradation that had the power to exasperate her almost to the verge of despair.[29]

The absolute lack of a positive energy in the dependent peoples to help themselves is one of the most discouraging aspects of the negative side to the "burden". All they seem to be able to do is complain and talk. One example of Conrad's subconscious realization of this appears in an unrelated remark in a passage describing Brierly: " 'Why eat all that dirt?' he exclaimed, with an Oriental energy of expression – about the only sort of energy you can find a trace of east of the fiftieth meridian." [30] Even at the time of all the commotion among the officers on board the bridge

27 "An Outpost of Progress", in *Tales of Unrest*, p. 100.
28 *Nostromo: A Tale of the Seaboard*, p. 88.
29 *Ibid.*, p. 109.
30 *Lord Jim*, p. 66.

of the floundering *Patna*, one of the two native helmsmen "says he thought nothing" when asked about the incident by the court. The other helmsman at least went through some form of thought process since "he had a knowledge of some evil thing befalling the ship". But no positive action, even of self-preservation, occurred. As he explains, ". . . there had been no order; he could not remember an order; why should he leave the helm?" [31] To his credit, or to the credit of his trust, he did not believe that the officers were abandoning the ship to save their lives. As far as he was concerned he never would believe they abandoned for that reason; they must have done it for some other purpose. Such complete willingness to dump their lives into the white man's lap leads to an even further demoralization than the original state. When energy is necessarily demanded of them by the white man's attempting to better their condition, the response is almost always a negative display of vigor. Heyst's attempt to bring prosperity to the islands by the establishment of a coal-mining company is met by puny opposition, in the form of a branch barricade, from the natives of the mine area. " 'This', Heyst explained in his urbane tone, 'is a barrier against the march of civilization'." [32] The coal company failed, but the latent antagonism against betterment continued. "The advanced foot has been drawn back, but the barricade remains." [33]

Since the dependents realize they must turn to the whites for the source of constructively expended energy – symbolized by the passage from *Nostromo*: "Only the sala of the Casa Gould flung out defiantly the blaze of its four windows, the bright appeal of light in the whole dumb obscurity of the street." [34] – most all activity of administration is resigned to the white man. There was no question raised when Jim took over the problem of saving the Bugis community under Doramin, even though it meant war. Jim's remark to Marlow is,

"All at once I saw what I had to do . . . "

[31]   *Ibid.*, p. 98.
[32]   *Victory*, p. 344.
[33]   *Idem.*
[34]   *Nostromo: A Tale of the Seaboard*, p. 187.

There was no doubt that it had come to him; and it had come through the war, too, as is natural, since this power that came to him was the power to make peace. It is in this sense alone that might so often *is* right.[35]

But this "right" – a justification of British military force – was not enough. Although all he did was for the salvation of the Bugis people, "when he got an idea he had to drive it into reluctant minds, through the bulwarks of fear, of selfishness". When he had succeeded in this much he had completed only the minor part of his task. In every case it was he, he who

had to devise the means. He devised them – an audacious plan; and his task was only half done. He had to inspire with his own confidence a lot of people who had hidden and absurd reasons to hang back; he had to conciliate imbecile jealousies, and argue away all sorts of senseless mistrusts.[36]

From the little affairs in bussiness, such as Vinck's over-seeing the Chinese money-counters, to the plans for a regained state, necessity for white supervision dominates. Lingard tells Jörgenson, "It would be better if I had a white man over there to look after things generally. There is a good lot of stores and arms – and Belarab would bear watching – no doubt." [37] No doubt.

In such an arrangement there can be no true liberty for the dependent ones. The paradox lies in the fact that their closest realization of independence and power results from dependence. Lakamba finally gains control of Sambir by bringing in the Dutch as masters: "With a faint rustle of trees, the breeze came down in light puffs, playing capriciously for a time with this [flag of the Netherlands] emblem of Lakamba's power, that was also a mark of his servitude. ..." [38]

The "virtue" most repugnant, after the "virtue" of the East's mistreatment of her own, is that shown in her reaction to the white man's response to her "brazen claims and dishonest hopes." [39]

Just before and during the attack and sack of Almayer's com-

---

[35] *Lord Jim*, p. 261.
[36] *Idem*.
[37] *The Rescue*, p. 103.
[38] *Almayer's Folly*, p. 132.
[39] *The Nigger of the Narcissus*, p. 4.

pound and trading station, his own followers deserted him with little if any compunction. His complaint and judgment are justified:

"They know no gratitude. How many times haven't I saved this settlement from starvation? Absolute starvation. Only three months ago I distributed again a lot of rice on credit. There was nothing to eat in this infernal place. They came begging on their knees. There isn't a man in Sambir, big or little, who is not in debt to Lingard & Co. Not one." [40]

This unbalance of attitude in give-and-take is intrinsic in Eastern peoples and is a charge made against each other, even among themselves. The perversion to which it can descend is truthfully portrayed in the person of Mahmat, to whom Almayer gives the free use of a house in his compound:

... he had made up his mind that if the white man ever wanted to eject him from his hut [Almayer had told him he himself might soon need the use of the house], he would burn it and also as many of the white man's other buildings as he could safely get at.[41]

Jörgenson is something of a monument to the ingratitude of the East. Far more valuable as an abstract example of the man of the "burden" than Almayer, he is brought far lower. He has devoted his life to them and they have sucked it from him. They have not even shown the foresight not to suck him dry so that he can be of continual use to them. Having exhausted him they toss his shell away. We have already seen to what depths he has sunk in "going native" and how the East subsequently rejected him. He had a deficiency at some point in his being to have failed, but we are led to believe that the deficiency was an excess of devotion to his sense of the "burden". He tells Lingard,

"They know me now – it's time – thirty-five years. Some of them give a plate of rice and a bit of fish to the white man. That's all I get – after thirty-five years – given up to them.
He was silent for a time.
"I was like you once", he added. . . .[42]

He speaks of his native wife: " 'That's the worst of all', he said with slow emphasis. 'That's the end. I came to them from the

---

[40]   *An Outcast of the Islands*, p. 171.
[41]   *Ibid.*, p. 318.
[42]   *The Rescue*, p. 100.

other side of the earth and they took me and – see what they
made of me.' " [43] Even though we feel that Jörgenson is not
wholly without fault, we cannot help considering that his over-
indulgence in one Anglo-Saxon "virtue" was ruthlessly taken
advantage of by the East. Such is her nature.

The doubt and hopelessness of final success in instilling Anglo-
Saxon concepts of virtue into the Orient is frankly declared in a
letter from Marlow about Jim, in which the unknown recipient
himself is quoted:

You prophesied for him the disaster of weariness and of disgust with
acquired honour, with the self-appointed task, with the love sprung
from pity and youth. You had said you knew so well "that kind of
thing", its illusory satisfaction, its unavoidable deception. You said
also – I call to mind – that "giving your life up to them" (them
meaning all of mankind with skins brown, yellow, or black in colour)
"was like selling your soul to a brute". You contended that "that kind
of thing" was only endurable and enduring when based on a firm conviction in the truth of ideas racially our own, in whose name are
established the order, the morality of an ethical progress. "We want
its strength at our backs", you had said. "We want a belief in its
necessity and its justice, to make a worthy and conscious sacrifice of
our lives. Without it the sacrifice is only forgetfulness, the way of
offering it is no better than the way to perdition." In other words,
you maintained that we must fight in the ranks or our lives don't
count. Possibly![44]

Marlow is often Conrad, but in this passage of credo we have the
core of the man. Taking into consideration the body of Conrad's
works, it is easy to arrive at the conclusion that this nameless
recipient of a letter from Marlow, unmentioned in any other place
in the story, can be none other than Conrad unfettered as a
character in a book. Taking the same material into account, we
have no doubts that the unnamed person's use of the word "want"
in connection with "its strength" and "a belief" is in the sense of
"desire" or "need", and not "lack". His use of the phrase "in the
ranks" does not exclude the idea of leading, but means among
those active in assuming the "burden". In his complex being of

[43] *Ibid.*, p. 104.
[44] *Lord Jim*, pp. 338-339.

part Conrad and part contra-Conrad, Marlow supplies the major proportion of reluctance in this passage.

Three other characters in his works display Conrad's sense of the slowly crushing somberness of the responsibility of the "burden". We have seen that Lingard does not like the long, involved talk of the natives when he is attempting to arrive at a situation's truth. But he allows Babalatchi to talk on and on, hoping

that from the talk a ray of light would shoot through the thick blackness of inexplicable treachery, to show him clearly – if only for a second – the man upon whom he would have to execute the verdict of justice. Justice only! Nothing was further from his thoughts than such a useless thing as revenge. Justice only. It was his duty that justice should be done. . . .

He was tolerant of all the talk, "and willingly dilatory, under the fearsome oppression of his call." [45]

The doer of justice sat with compressed lips and a heavy heart, while the calm darkness outside the silent world seemed to be waiting breathlessly for that justice he held in his hand – in his strong hand: – ready to strike – reluctant to move.[46]

Another man "under the fearsome oppression of his call", Charles Gould,

had gone forth into the senseless fray as his poor uncle, whose sword hung on the wall of his study, had gone forth – in the defense of the commonest decencies of organized society. Only his weapon was the wealth of the mine, more far-reaching and subtle than an honest blade of steel fitted into a simple brass guard.

More dangerous to the wielder, too, this weapon of wealth, double-edged with the cupidity and misery of mankind, steeped in all the vices of self-indulgence as in a concoction of poisonous roots, tainting the very cause for which it is drawn, always ready to turn awkwardly in the hand. There was nothing for it now but to go on using it.[47]

Emilia, his wife, says,

"Ah, if we had left it alone, Charley!"

"No", Charles Gould said, moodily; "it was impossible to leave it alone."

"Perhaps it was impossible", Mrs. Gould admitted slowly. Her lips

---

[45]   *An Outcast of the Islands*, p. 223.
[46]   *Ibid.*, p. 224.
[47]   *Nostromo: A Tale of the Seaboard*, p. 365.

quivered a little, but she smiled with an air of dainty bravado. "We have disturbed a good many snakes in that Paradise, Charley, haven't we?"

"Yes, I remember", said Charles Gould, "it was Don Pépé who called the gorge the Paradise of snakes. No doubt we have disturbed a great many. But remember, my dear, that it is not now as it was when you made that sketch." He waved his hand towards the small water-colour hanging alone upon the great bare wall. "It is no longer a Paradise of snakes. We have brought mankind into it, and we cannot turn our backs upon them to go and begin a new life elsewhere." [48]

Lingard is exhausted and financially ruined by his long life of service to the "oppression of his call"; Charles Gould, possessor of a great white wall blank except for the picture-token of the short happy period of his early life with Emilia, has no other reward for his devotion to the "burden"; Emilia has nothing but a tiny doubt that her happiness "was impossible". She has lost her all, her husband, to duty. But these three strongest characters in Conrad's major works realize the eternal fact: the responsibility is defined and is to be assumed; once assumed it is never cast down. Chance has put them in position on the site of the duty, but the dignity of their own free will has moved them into the involvement. No power but death can release them from that entanglement. What appears to be a "Paradise" is filled with in-numerable "snakes"; that they know or will learn. But it does not change their situation. In this powerful pessimism, there is yet, considering all his works, the overwhelming and outshining "positive belief" which weighs the question in the favor of Conrad's – not reluctance, but conviction. Concerning the colonial philosophy as presented by Conrad, Captain Mitchell says far more than he imagines when he states, "A great power, this, for good and evil, sir. A great power." [49]

---

[48] *Ibid.*, p. 209.
[49] *Ibid.*, p. 486.

BIBLIOGRAPHY

Conrad, Joseph. *Complete Works*, twenty-five volumes (Garden City, New York, Doubleday, Page and Company, 1924):
Almayer's Folly
An Outcast of the Islands
Heart of Darkness, in *Youth*
Lord Jim
Nostromo: A Tale of the Seaboard
Notes on Life and Letters
The Mirror of the Sea
The Nigger of the Narcissus
The Rescue
The Secret Agent
Typhoon, in *Typhoon and Other Stories*
Under Western Eyes
Victory
"An Outpost of Progress", in *Tales of Unrest*
"Because of the Dollars", in *Within the Tides*
"Freya of the Seven Isles", in *'Twixt Land and Sea*
"Karain: A Memory", in *Tales of Unrest*
"The Lagoon", in *Tales of Unrest*
"The Planter of Malata", in *Within the Tides*

Dean, Leonard F., ed., *Joseph Conrad's "Heart of Darkness": Backgrounds and Criticisms* (Englewood Cliffs, N.J.: Prentice-Hall, Inc., 1960).
Guerard, Albert, Jr., "Joseph Conrad", *Directions*, Number 1 (New York, New Directions, 1947).
Harkness, Bruce, ed., *Conrad's "Heart of Darkness" and the Critics* (San Francisco, Wadsworth Publishing Company, Inc., 1960).
Hartman, Howard, *The Seas Were Mine* (London, George G. Harrap and Company, Ltd., 1936).
Sherry, Norman, *Conrad's Eastern World* (London, Cambridge Univ. Press, 1966).
Tindall, William York, *Forces in Modern British Literature 1885-1956* (New York, Vintage Books, 1956).